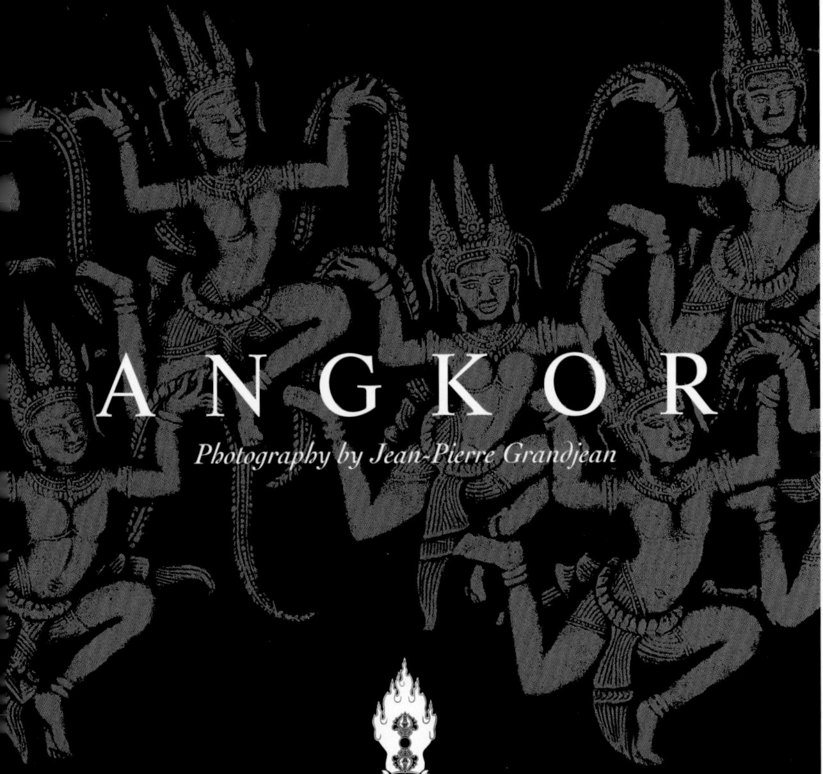

ANGKOR

Photography by Jean-Pierre Grandjean

SHAMBHALA

Boston 2002

Strange light today. Rain-colored sky. A silence broken by the flight of bats. Mysterious Ta Prohm as darkness sets in. Eternal stare of the repeated heads of the Bayon. Conniving smiles of the Apsaras. Capturing these marvels, in black and white, in color. Immortalizing, in fractions of seconds, centuries of history buried in this jungle.

— *Jean-Pierre Grandjean*

In the ninth century CE, the Khmer King Yashovarman I founded Angkor, the holy city that was to become the center of the Khmer empire for more than 500 years. Under Yashovarman and his successors, Angkor grew into a vast complex of temples, palaces, causeways, and reservoirs in an area covering about 100 square miles.

The monumental Angkor Wat was built in the twelfth century as a temple to the god Vishnu. The temple's towers, walls, and moats represent in microcosm the universe as conceived in Hindu cosmology. Its narrative bas reliefs celebrate the power of Angkor's king and depict tales of the gods, goddesses, and demons of Khmer mythology.

Angkor's King Jayavarman VII built the huge Bayon temple, which features 49 towers, each carved with four serene faces representing the bodhisattva Lokesvara. Jayavarman also built the great Buddhist temple-monastery Ta Prohm, where giant trees with sinuous roots have now overgrown the ruins and may ultimately destroy them.

In this book of photographs, Jean-Pierre Grandjean reveals the glories of Angkor, past and present—the decaying magnificence of its ancient monuments and the resilient spirit of the Khmer people who still worship at its ruins.

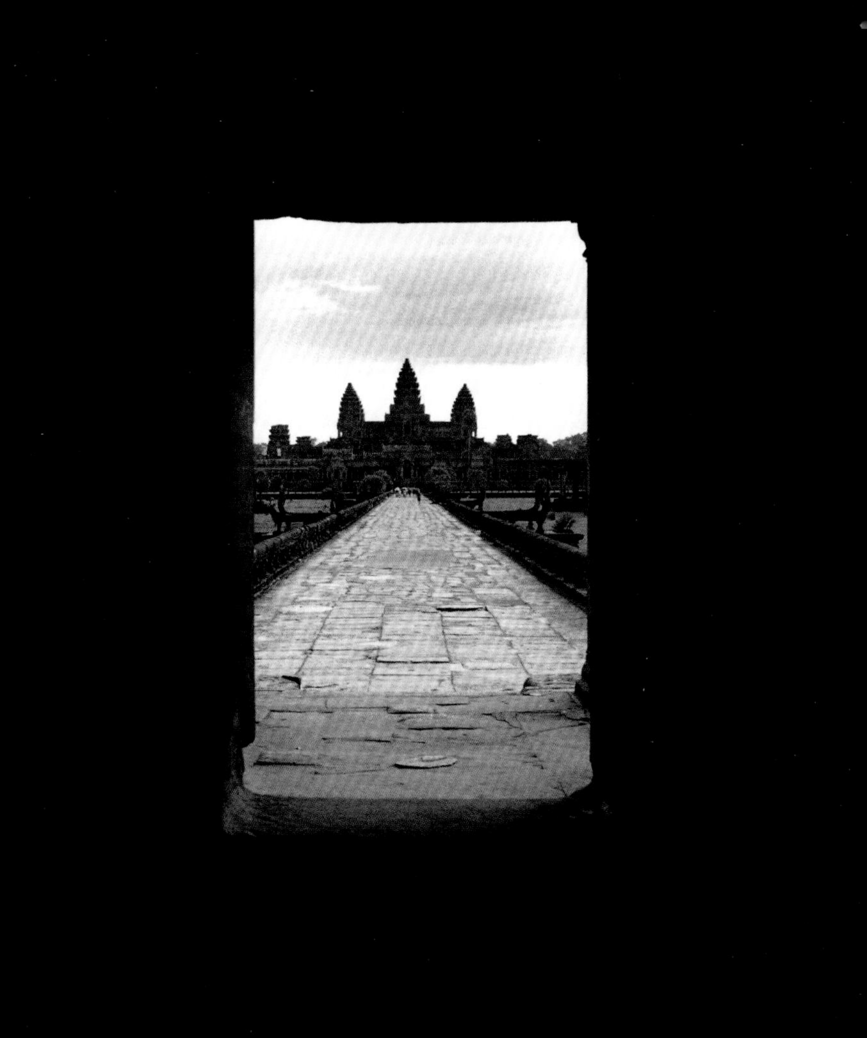

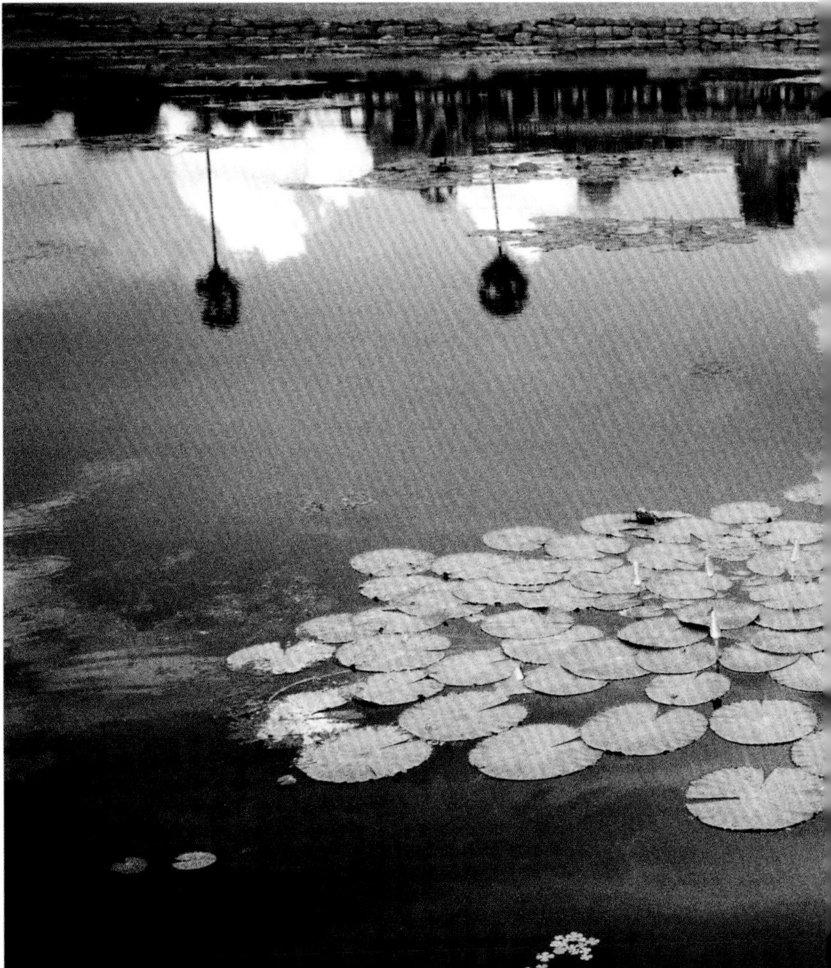

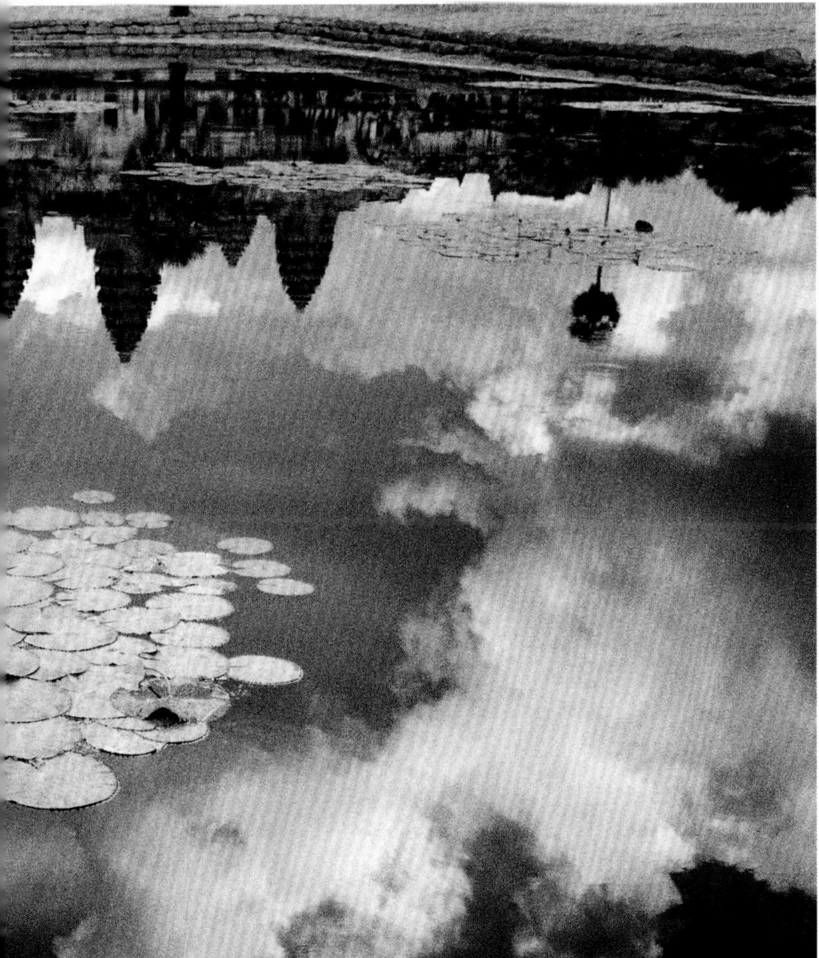

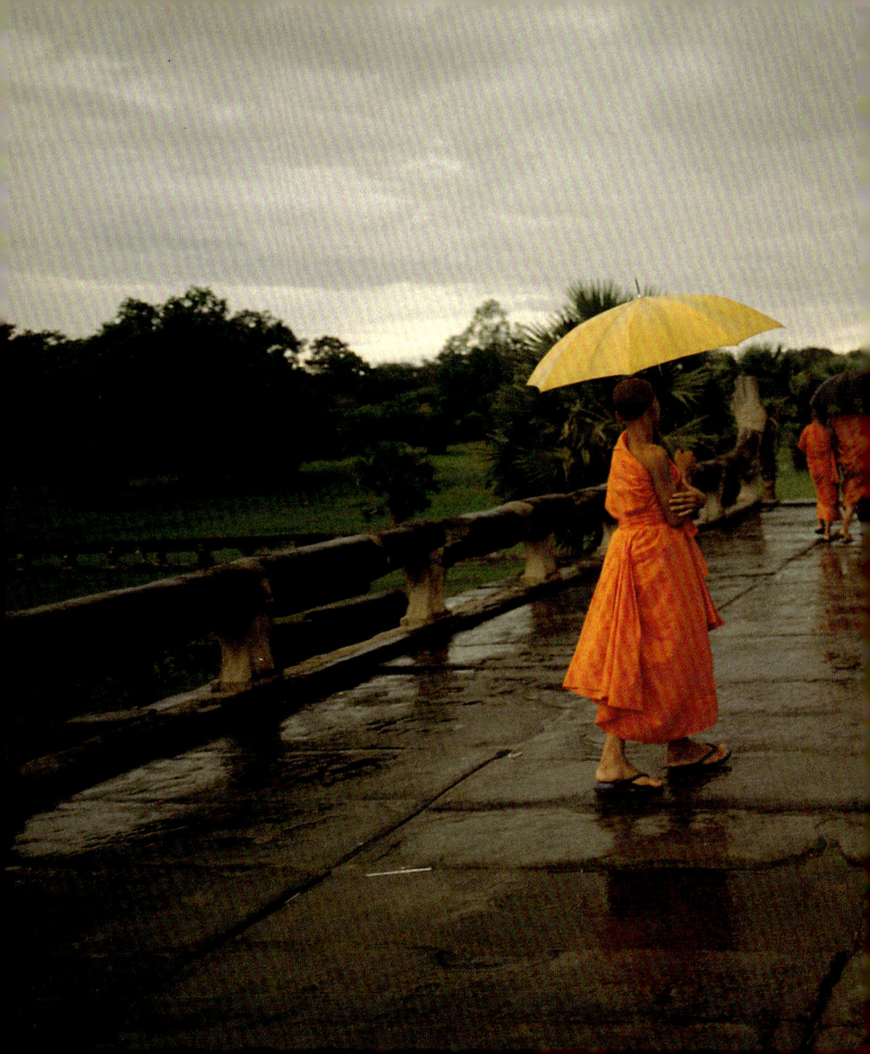

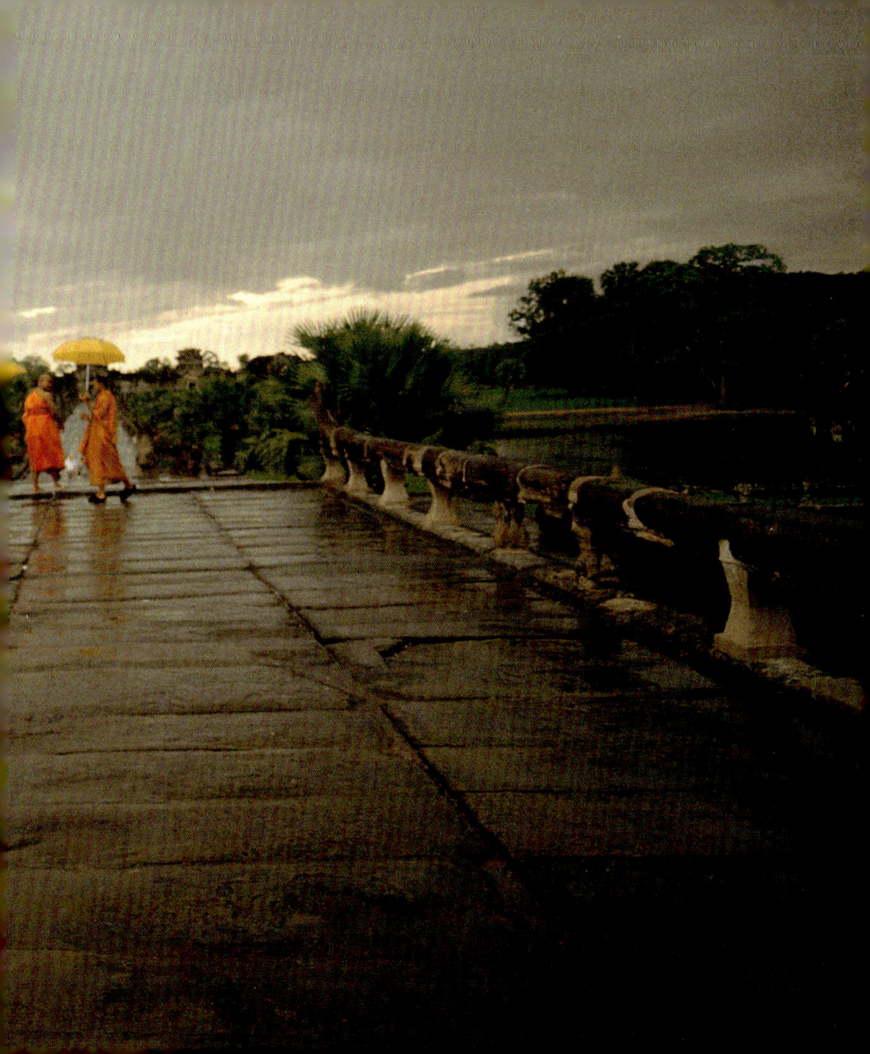

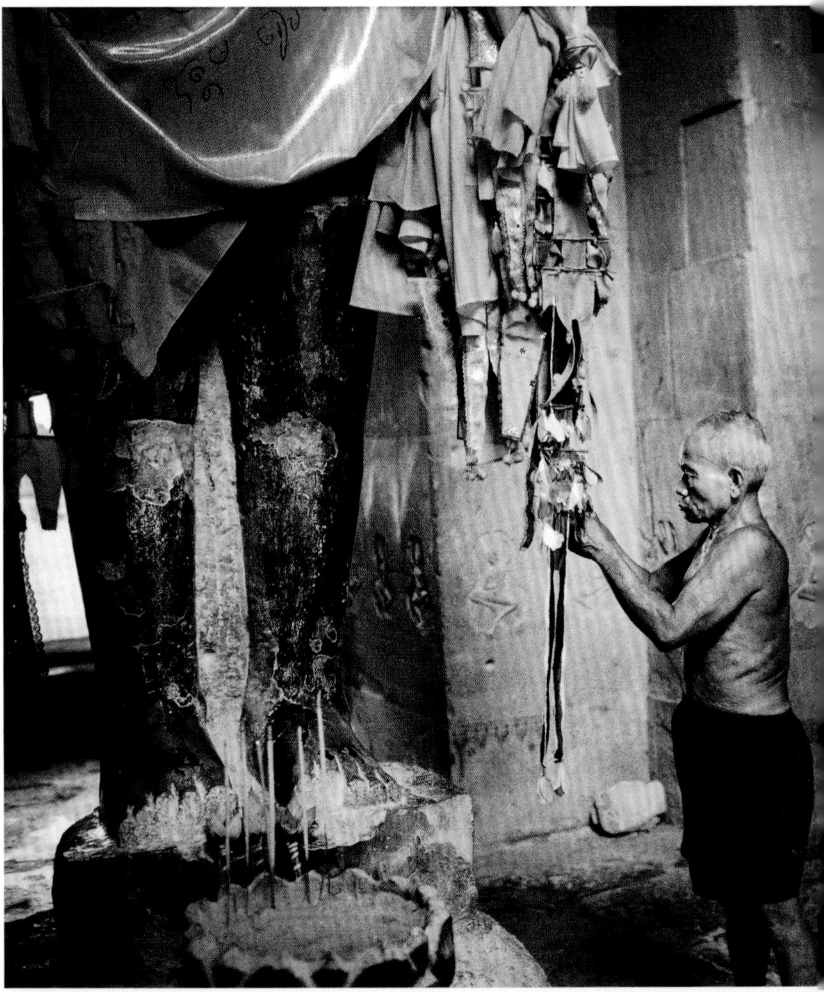

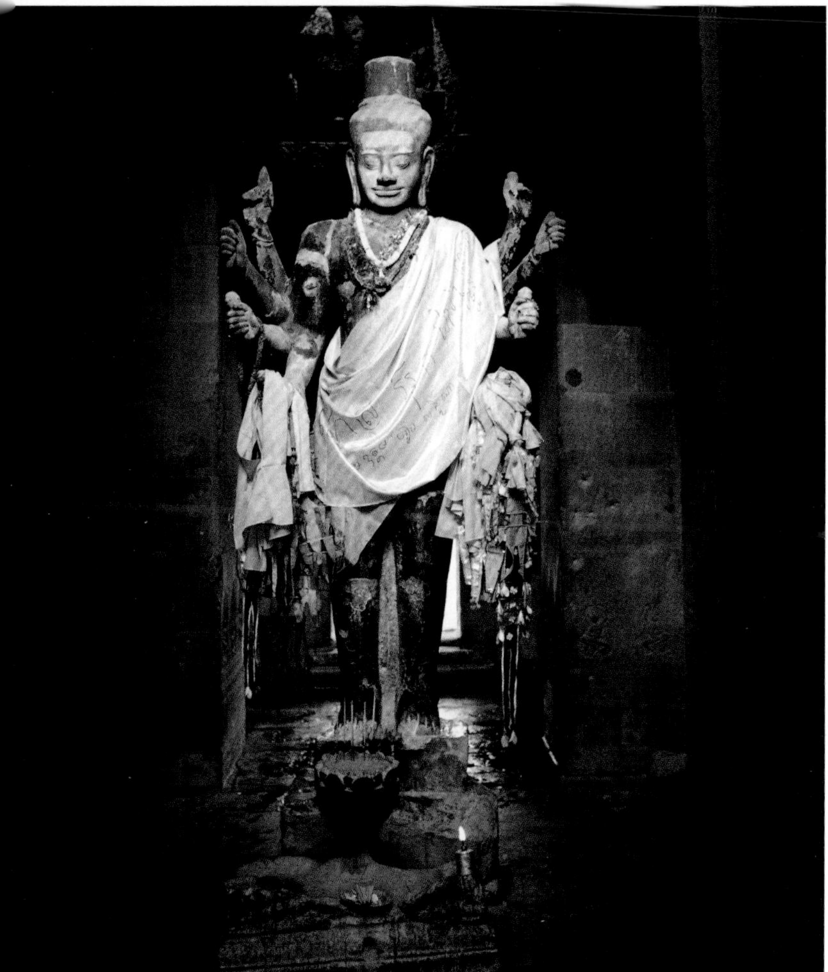

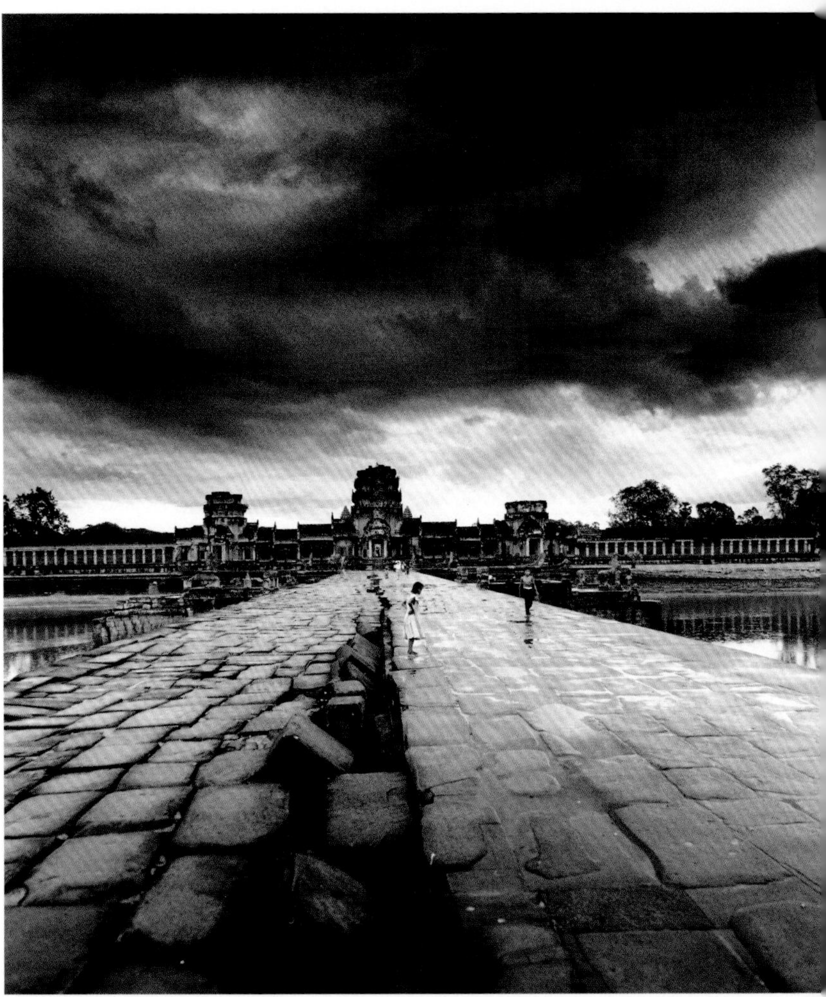

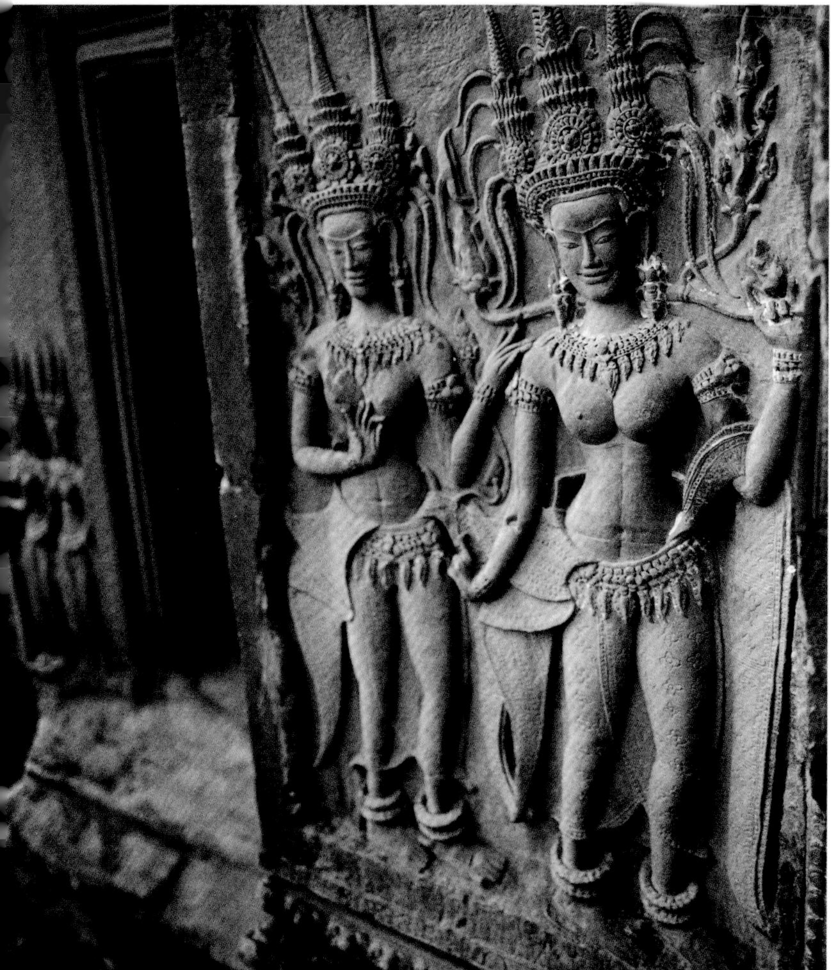

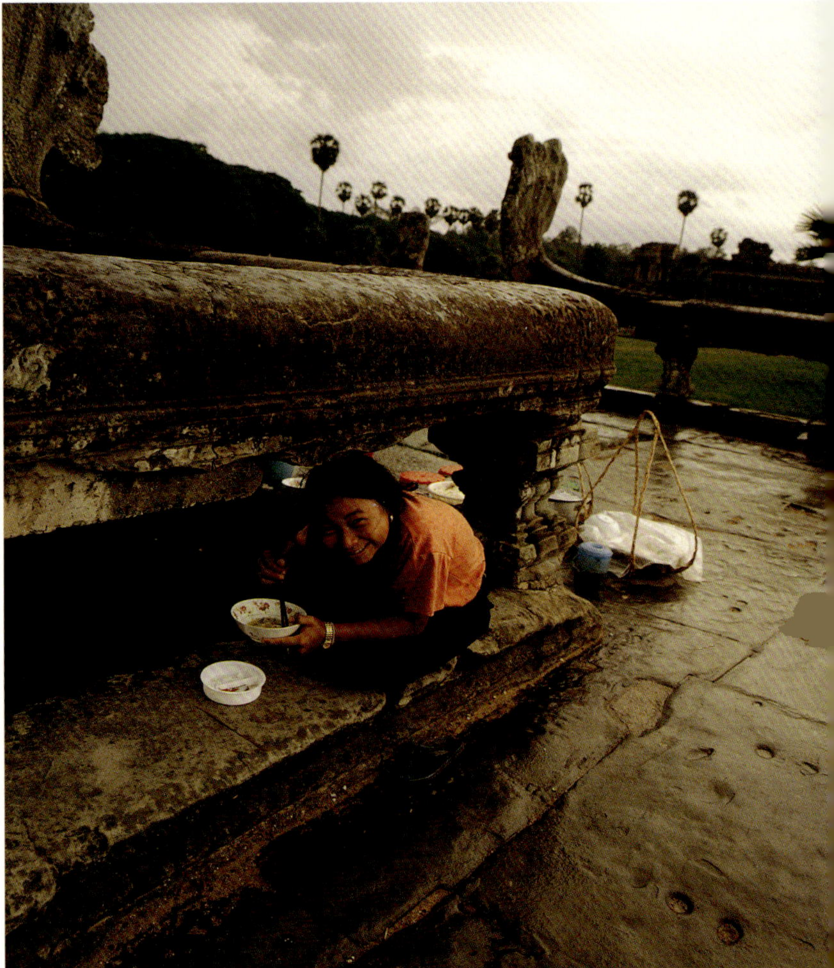

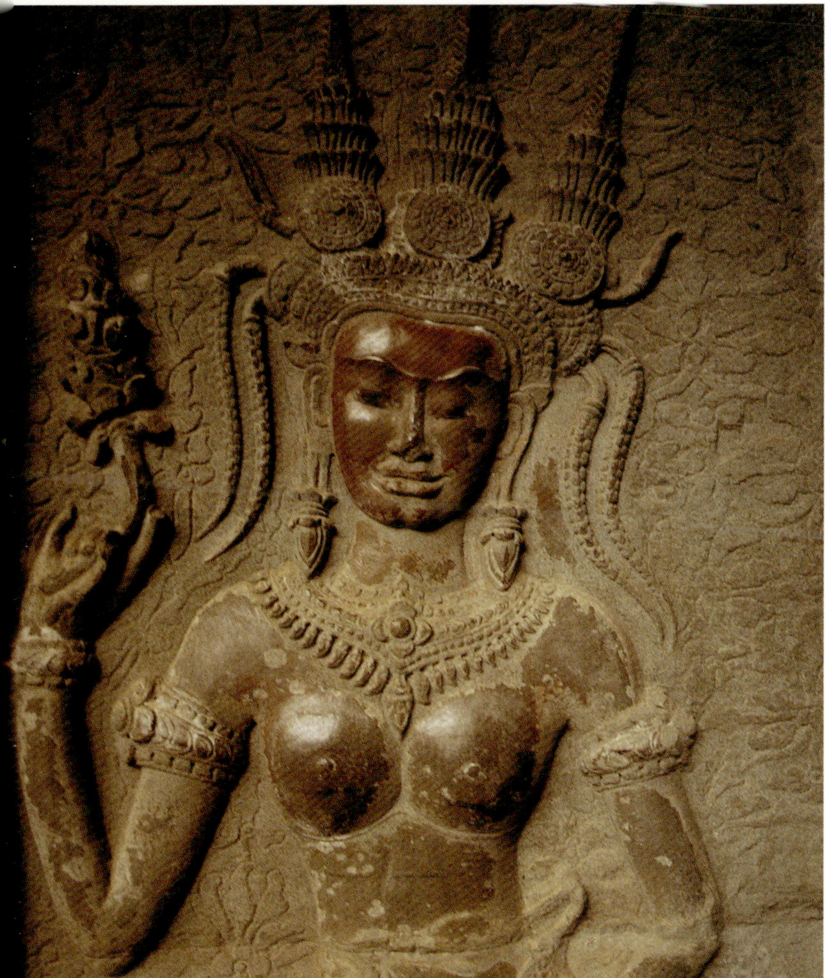

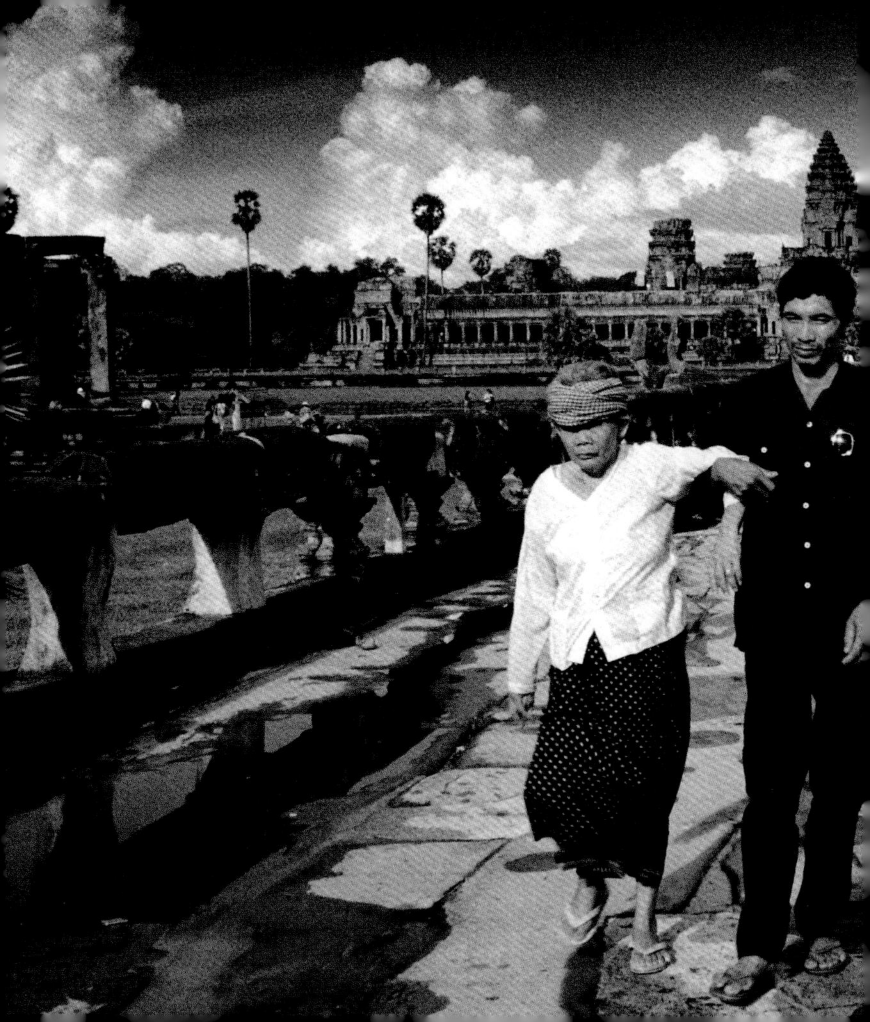

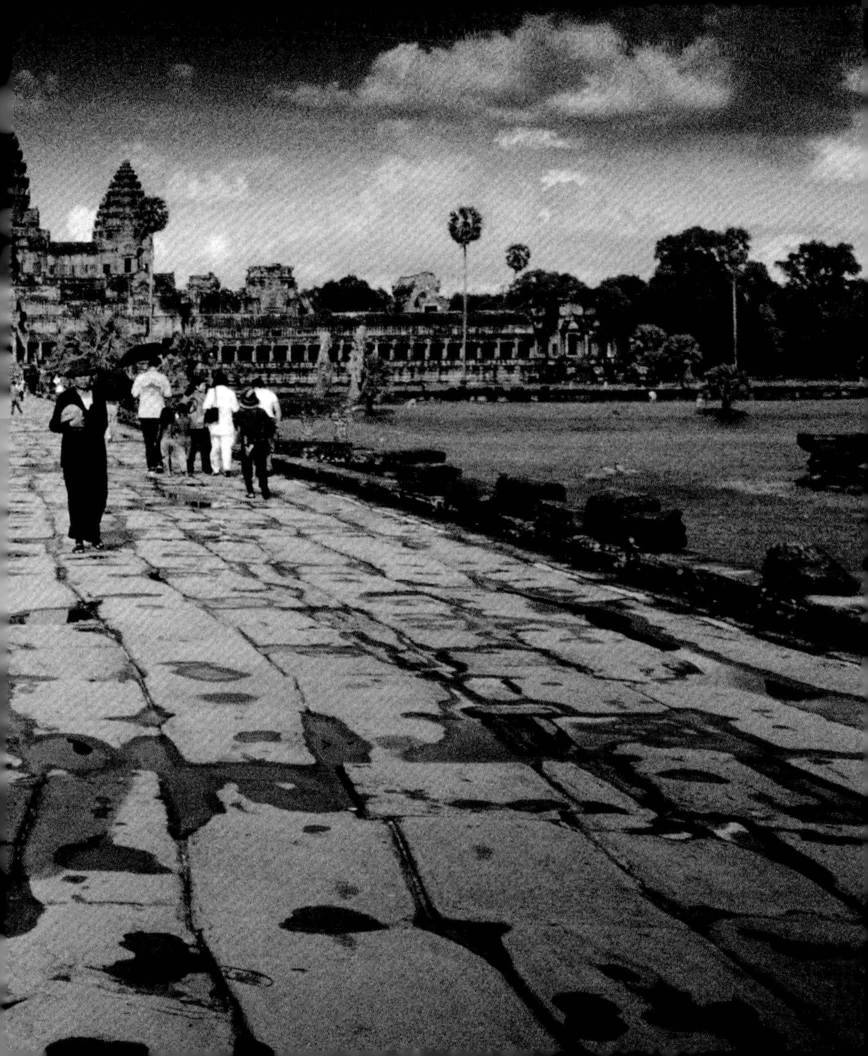

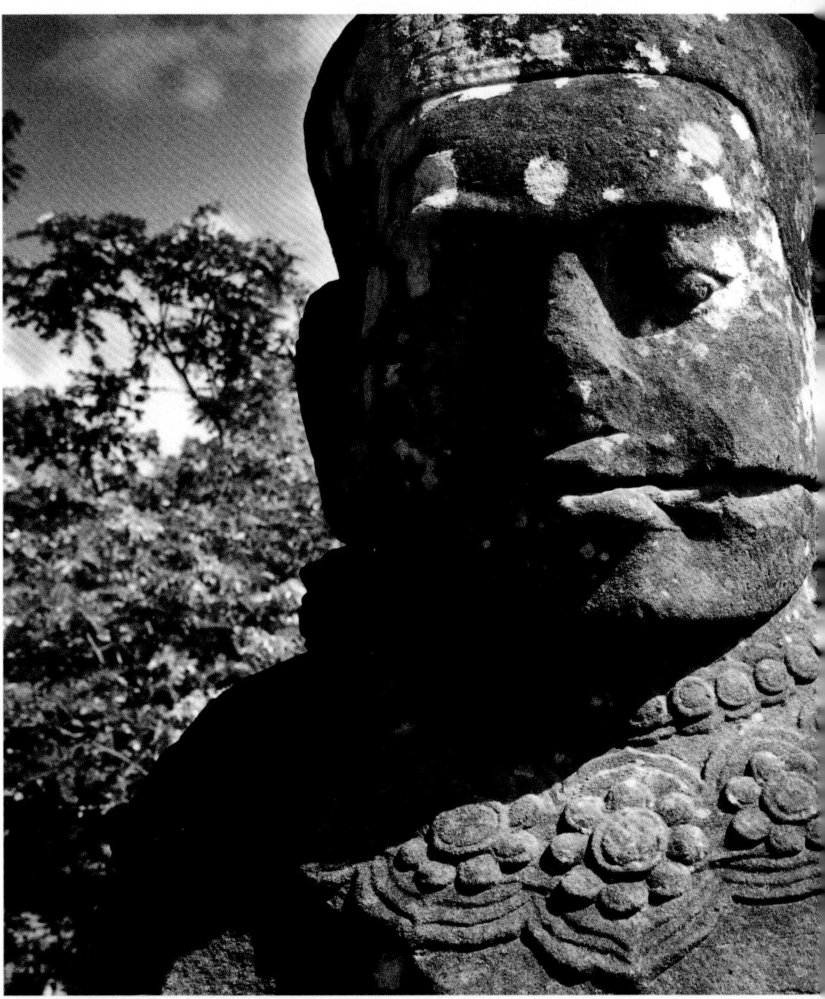

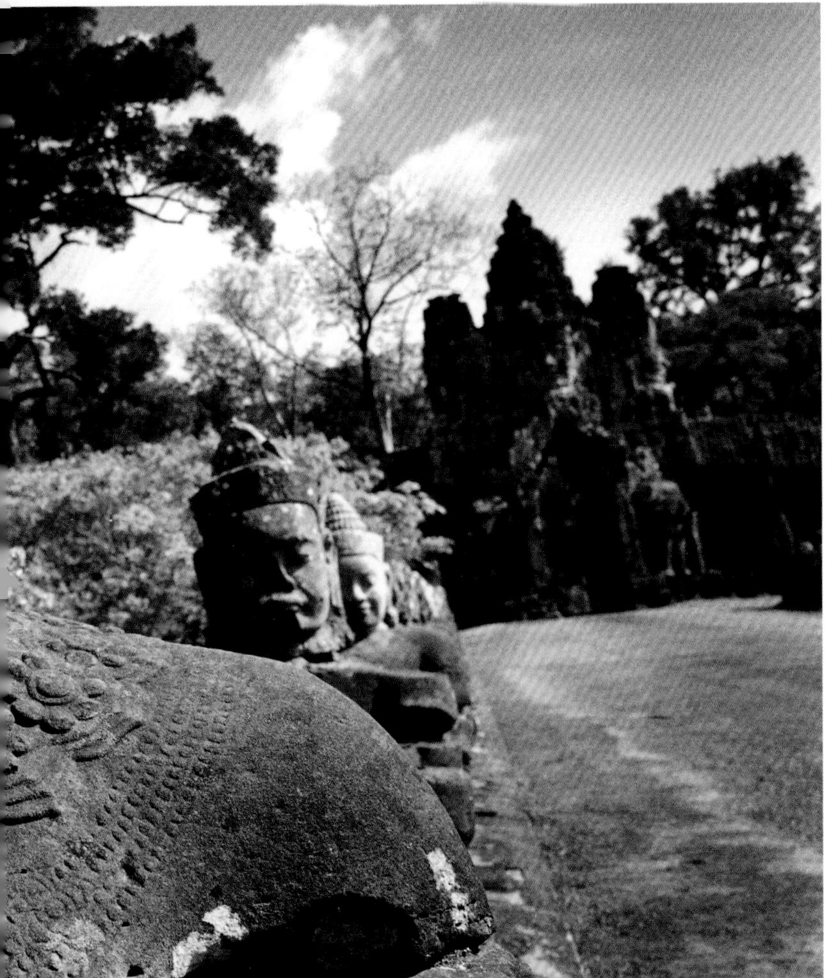

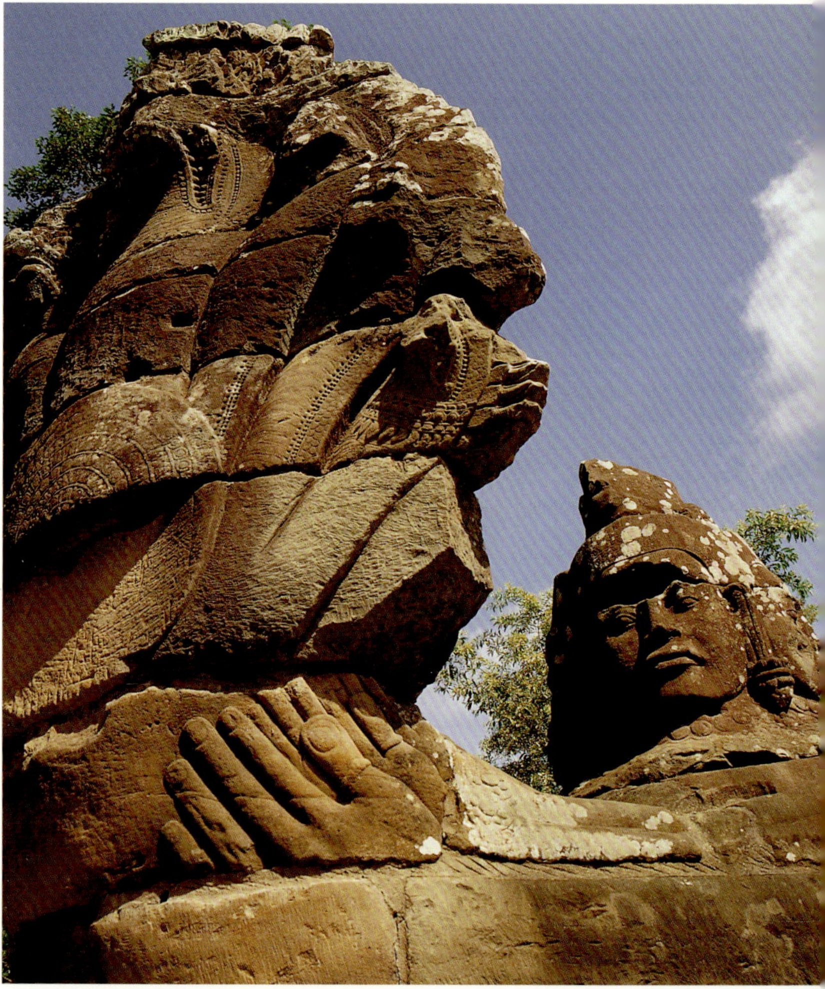

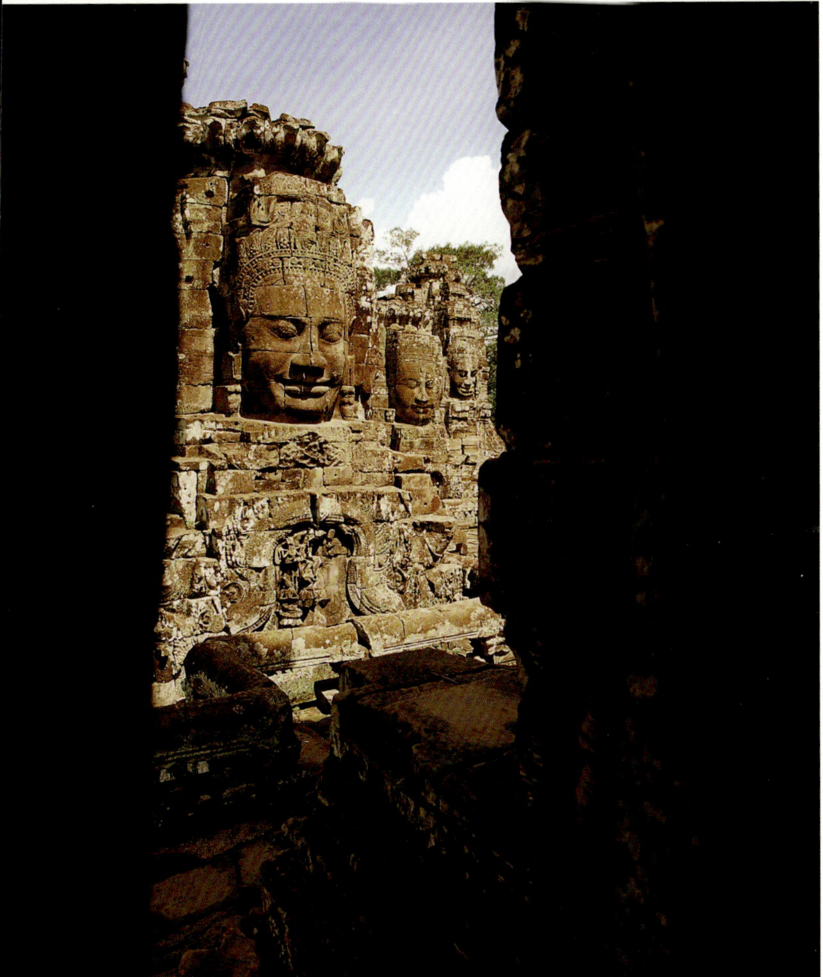

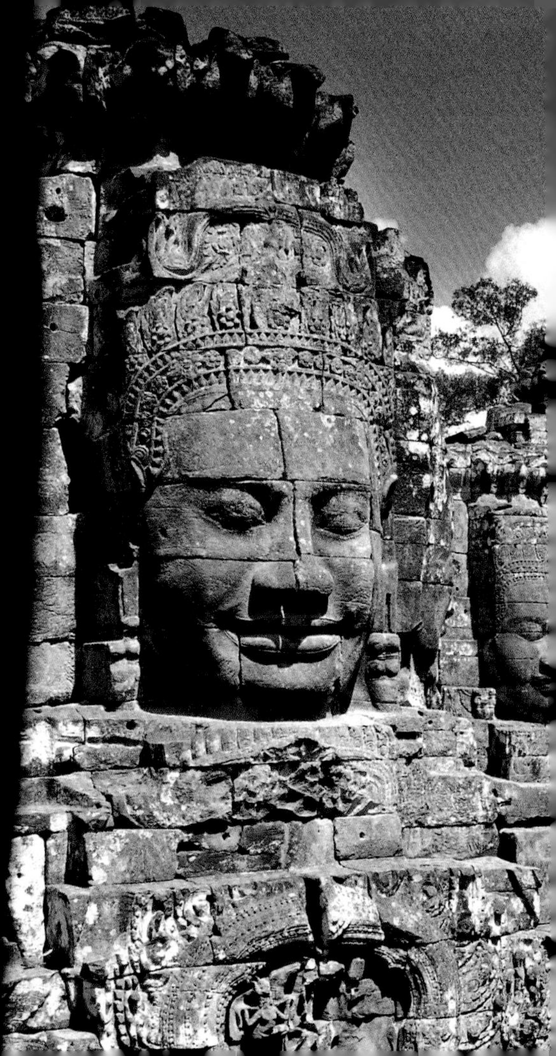

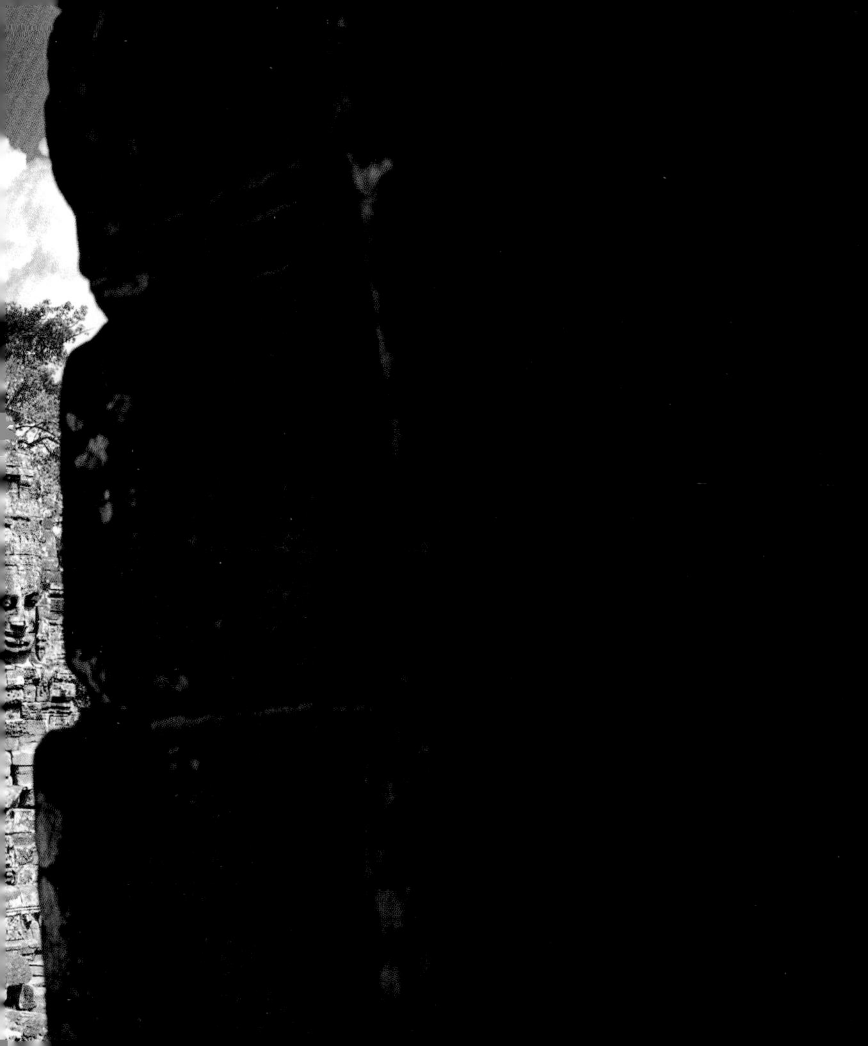

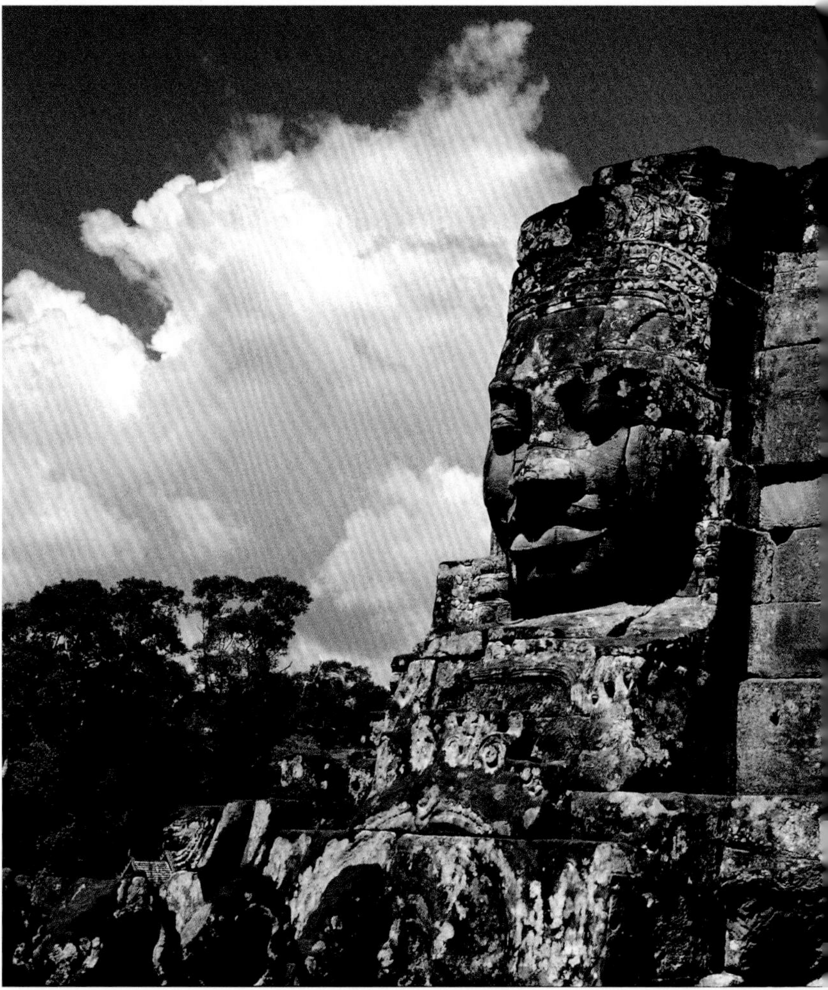

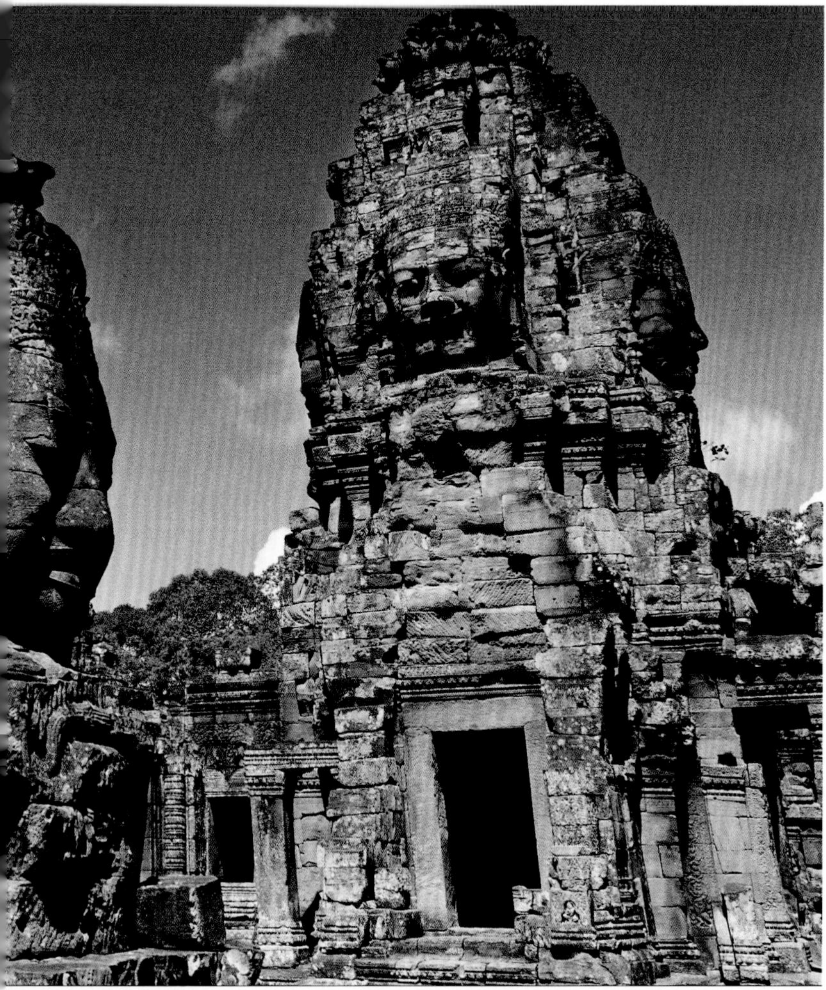

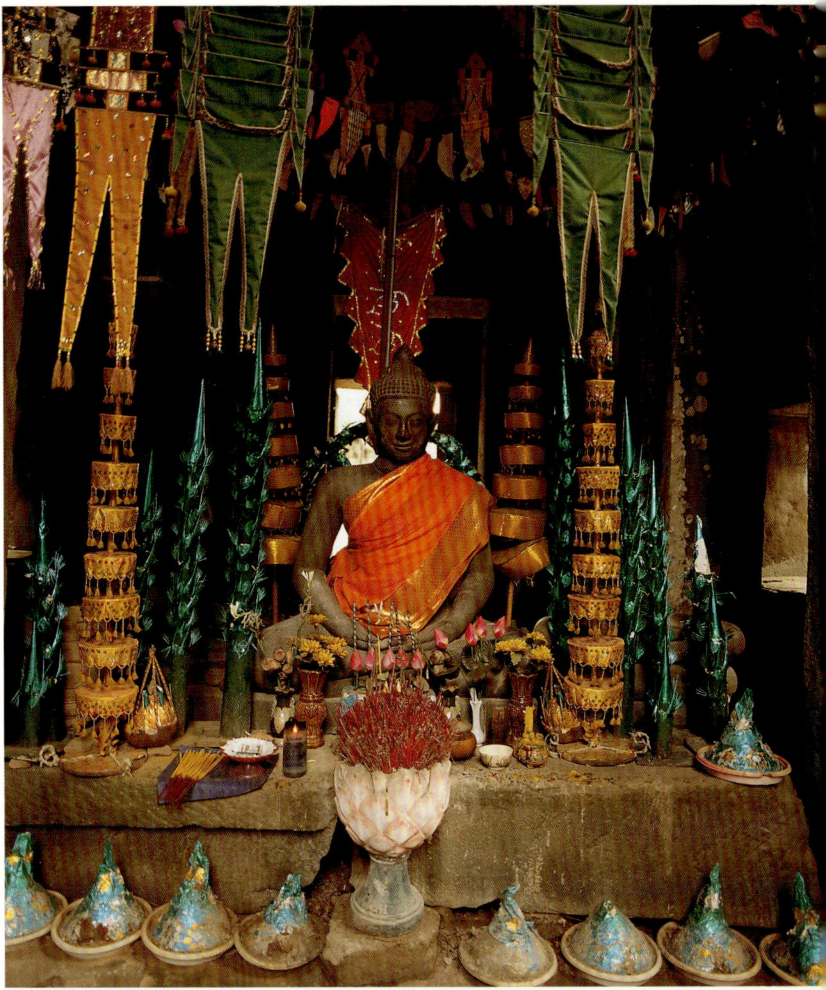

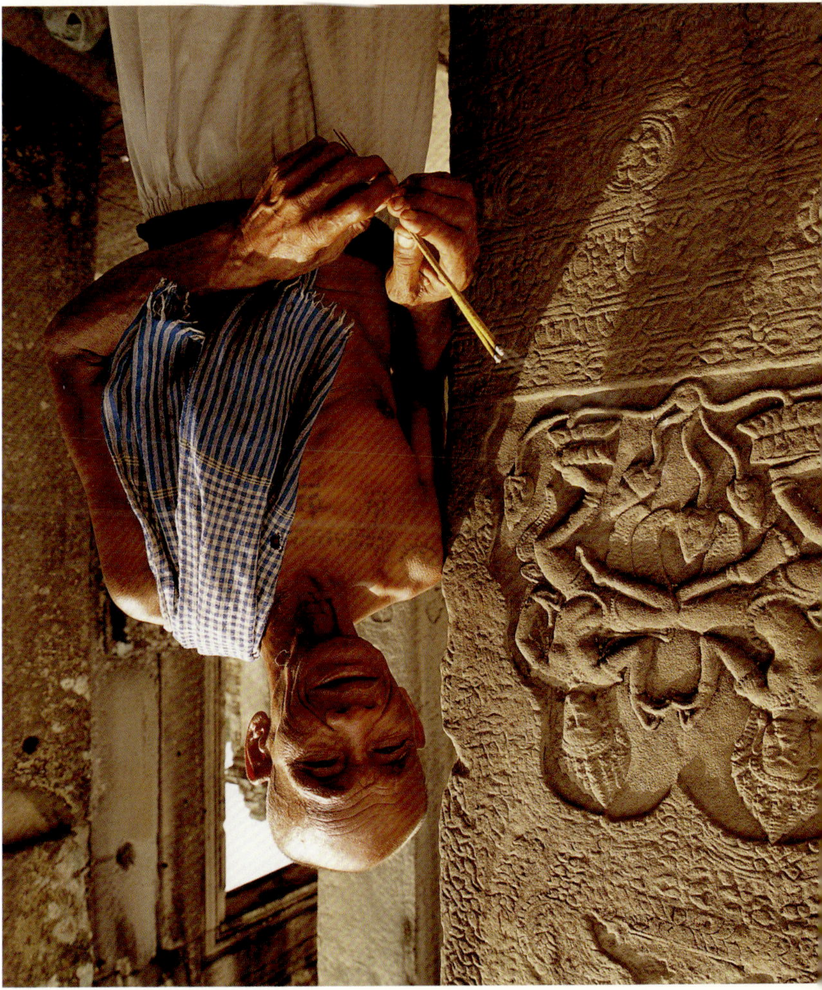

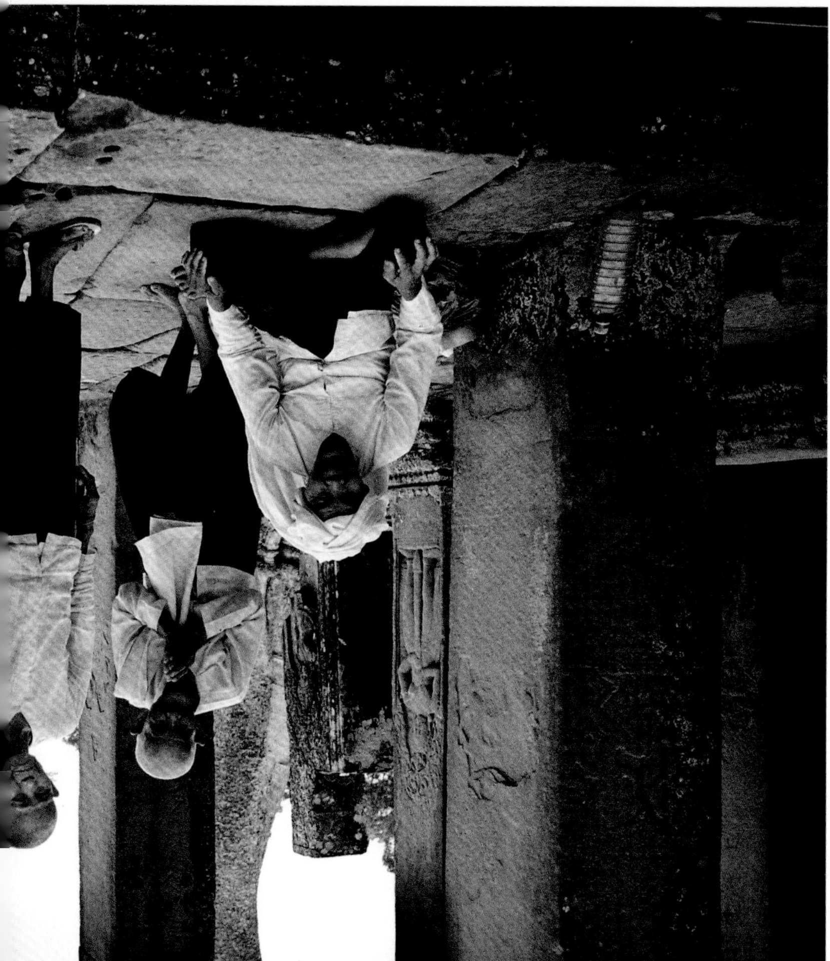

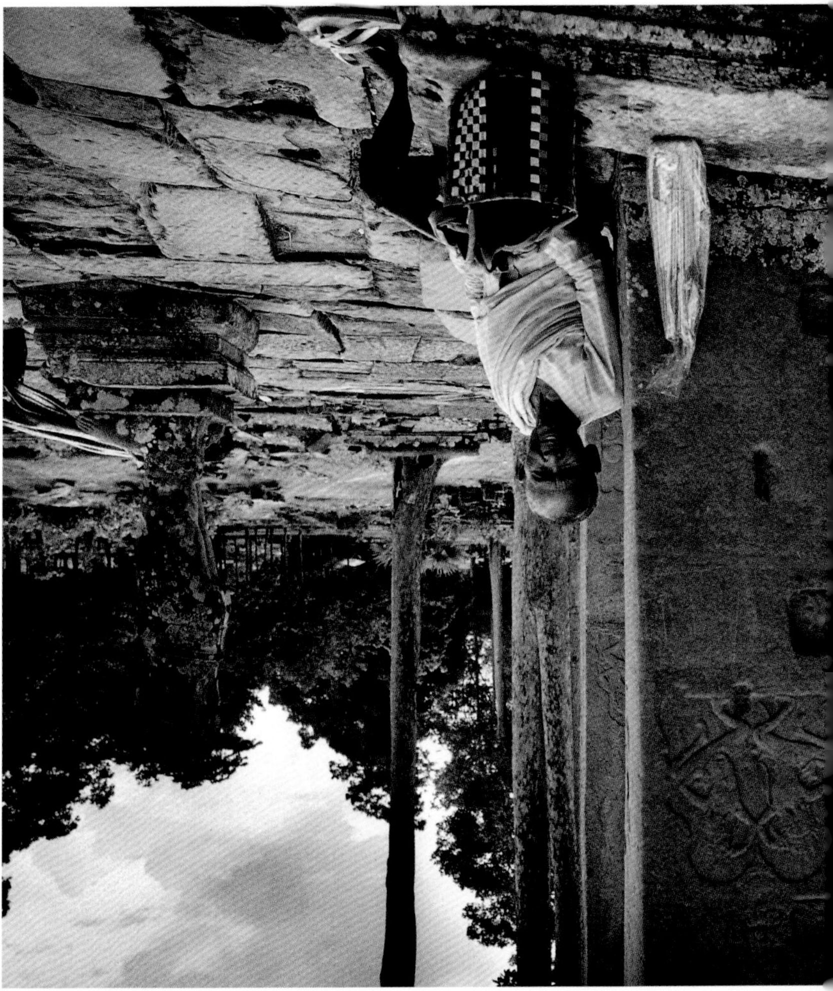

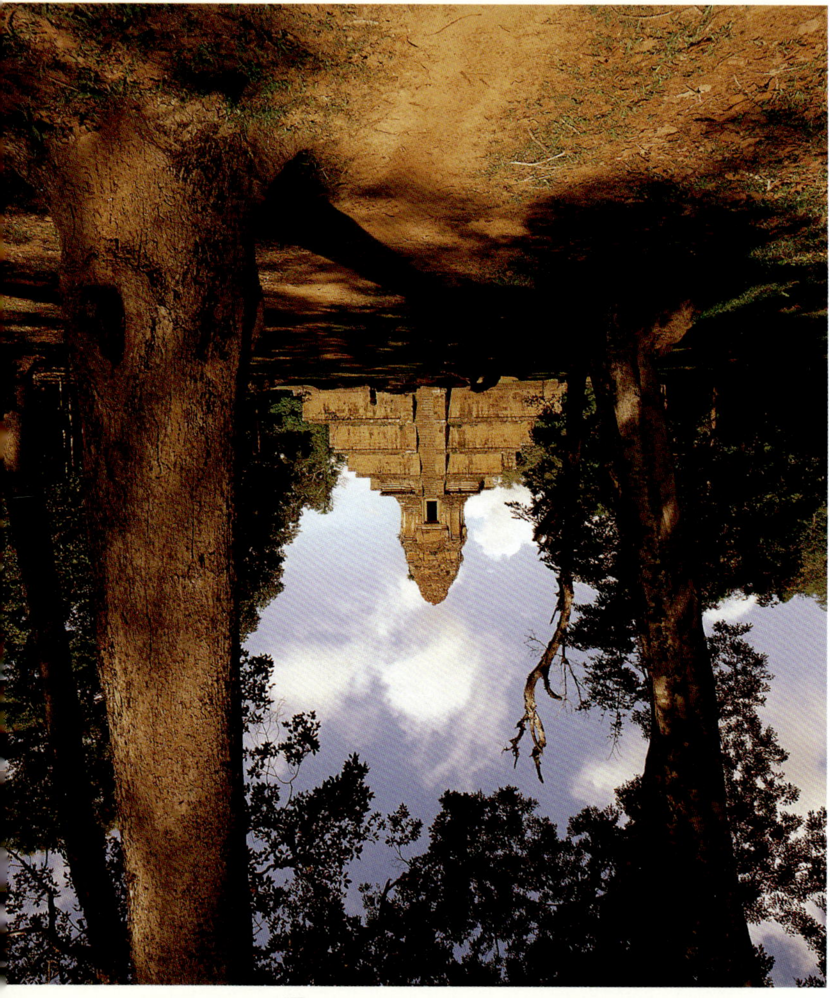

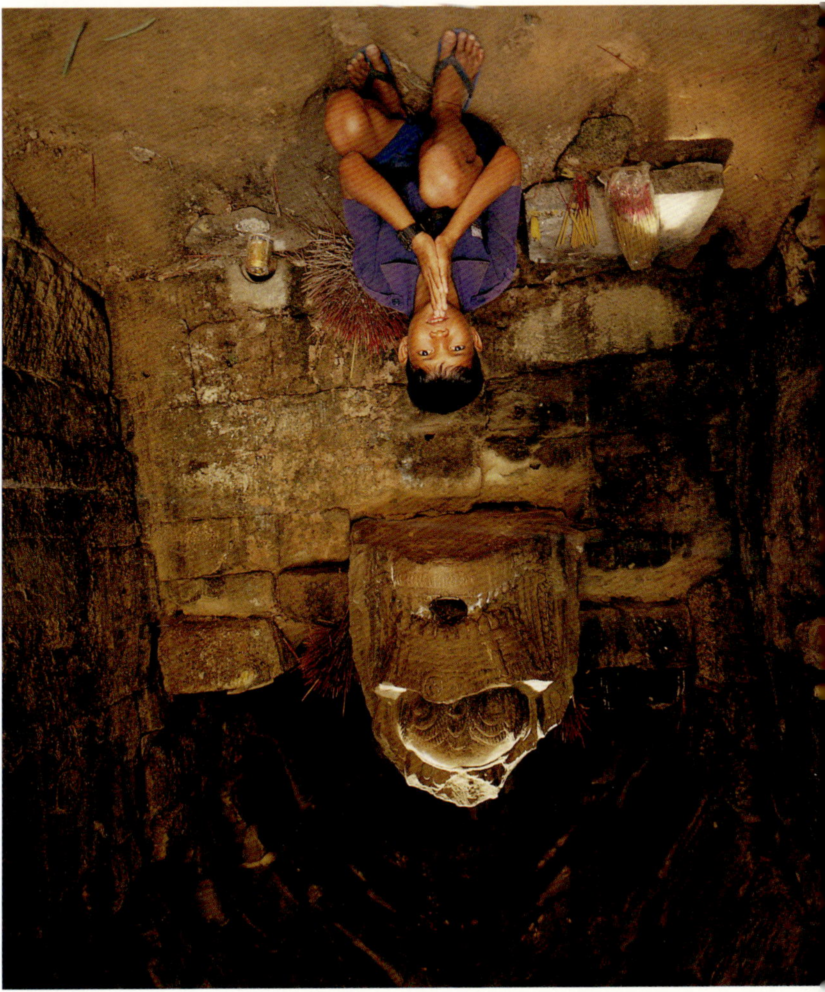

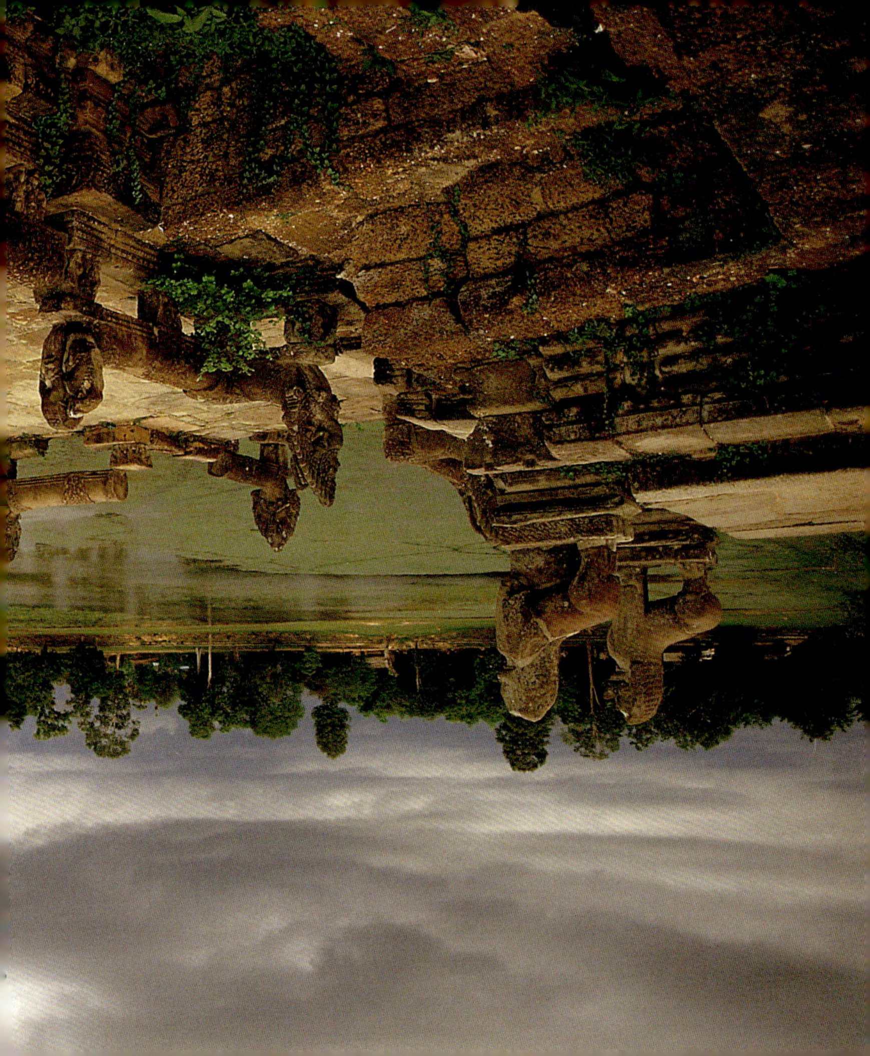

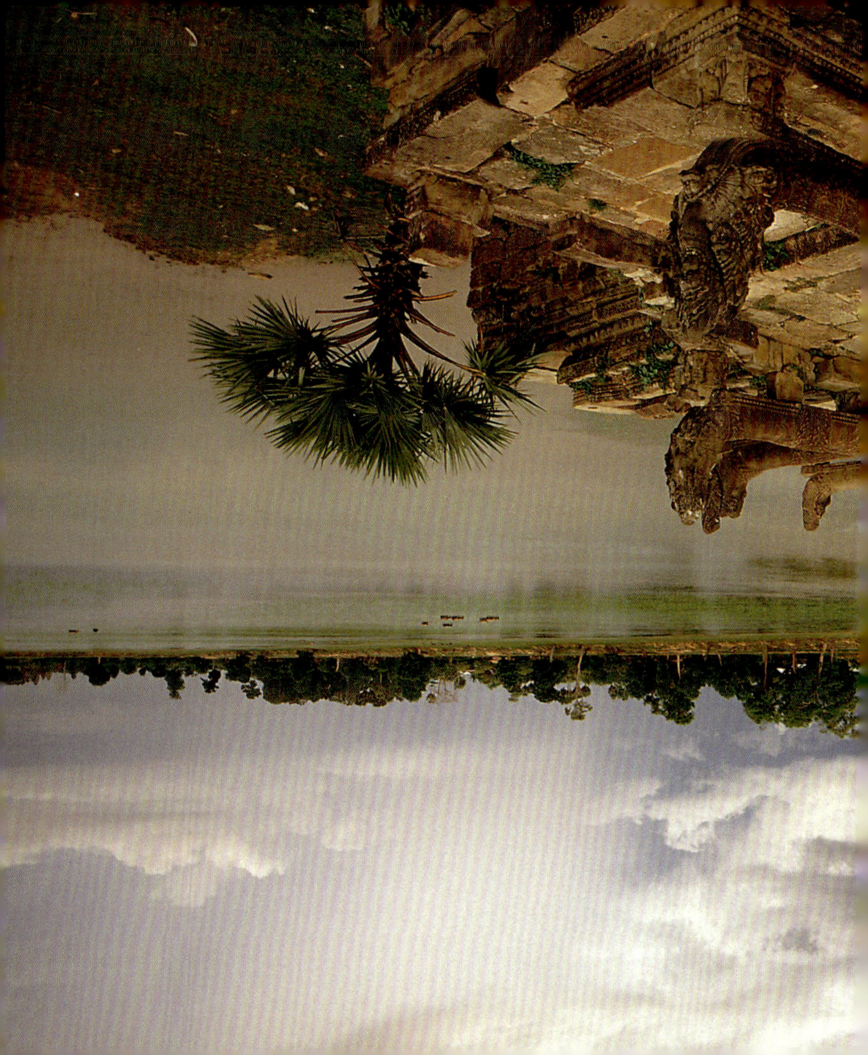

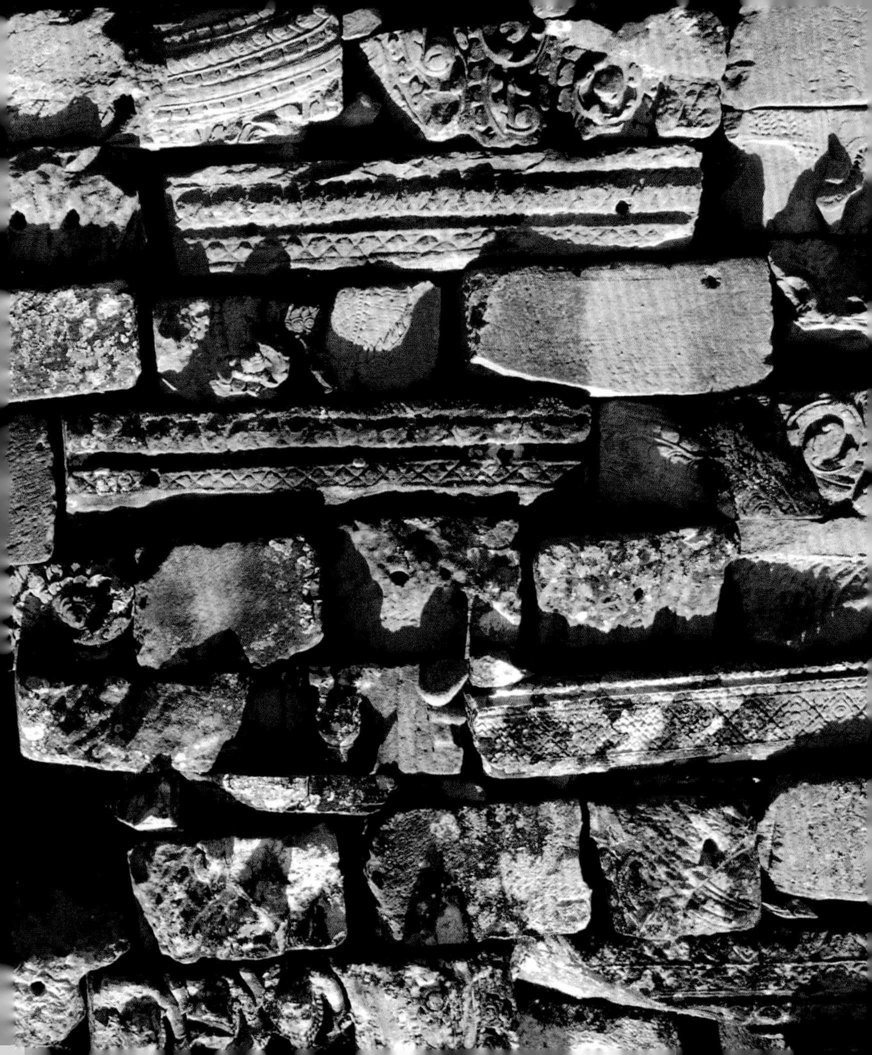

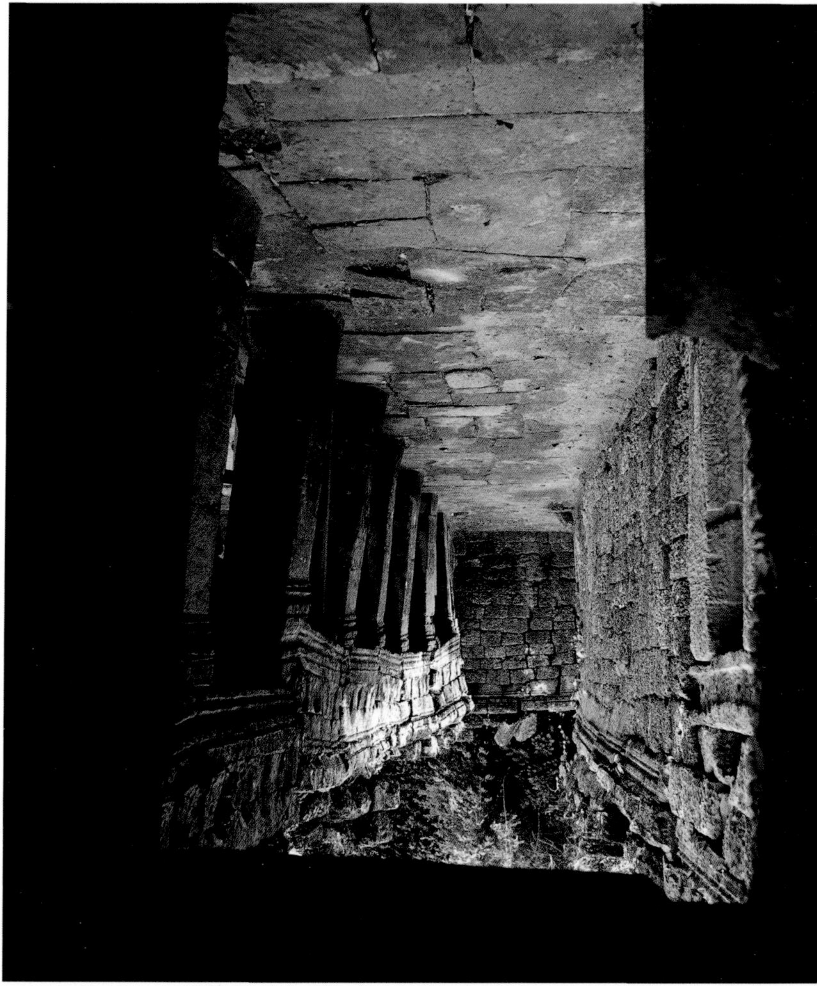

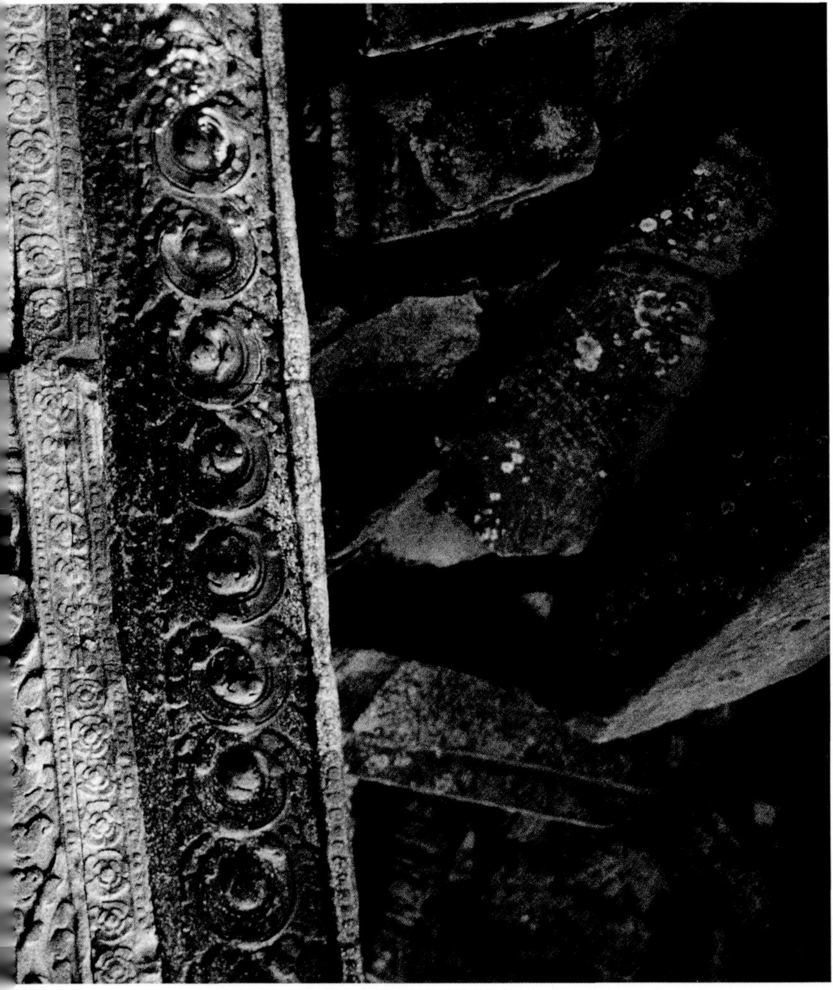

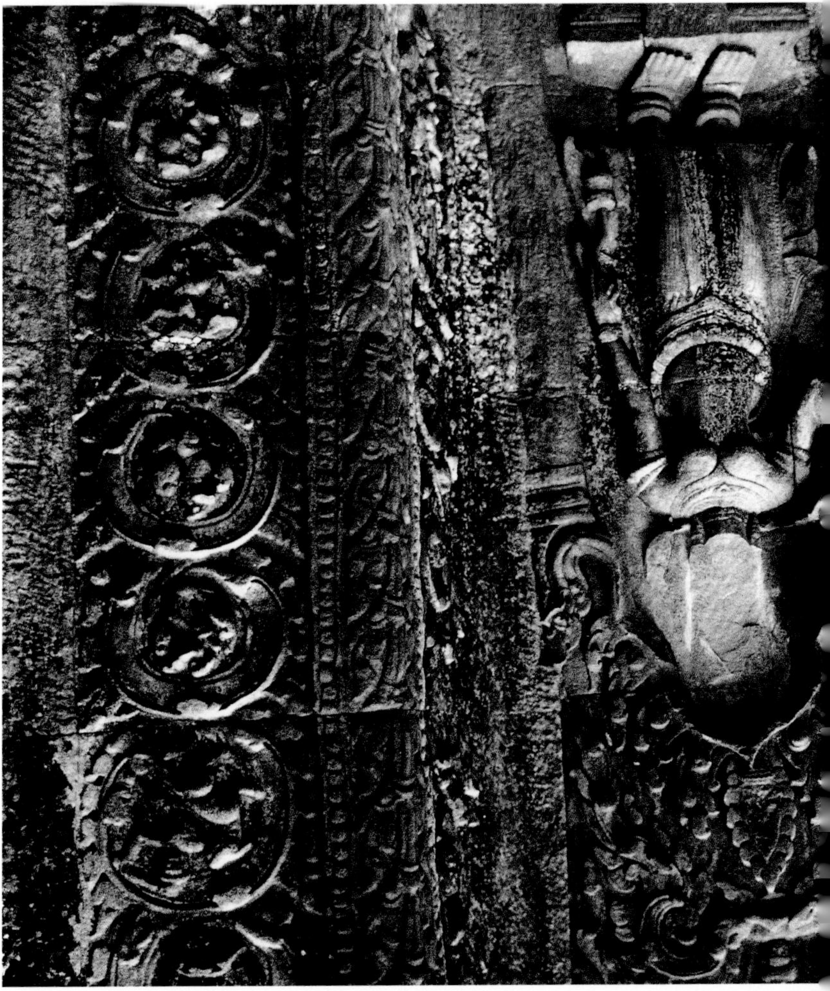

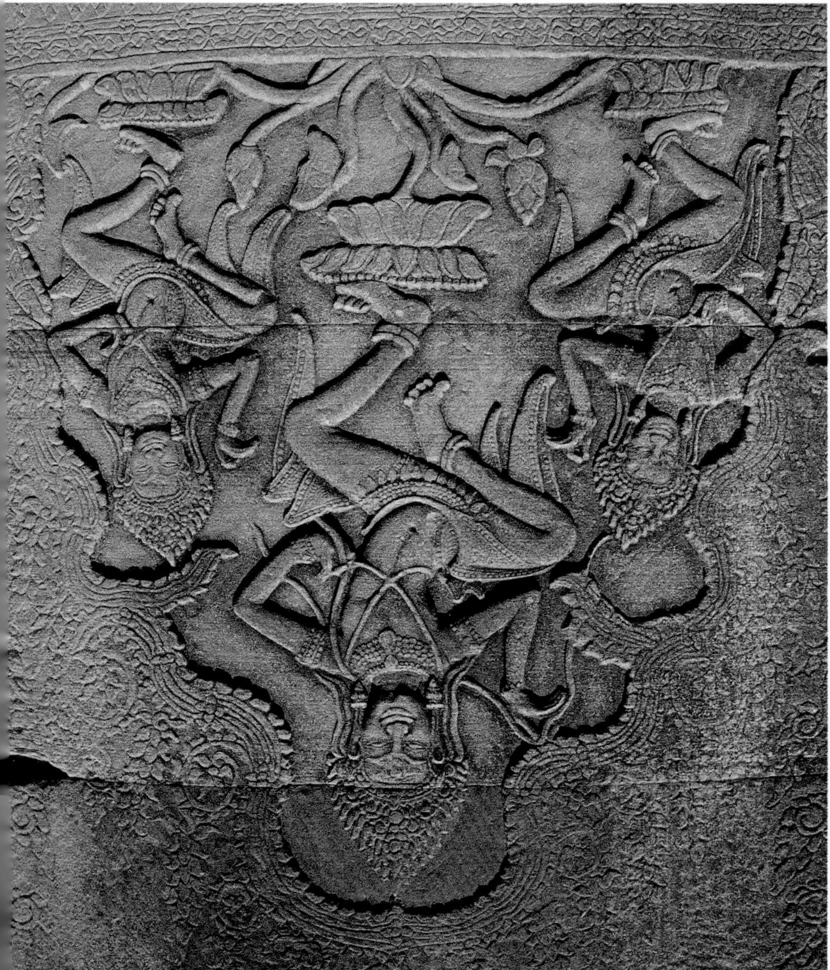

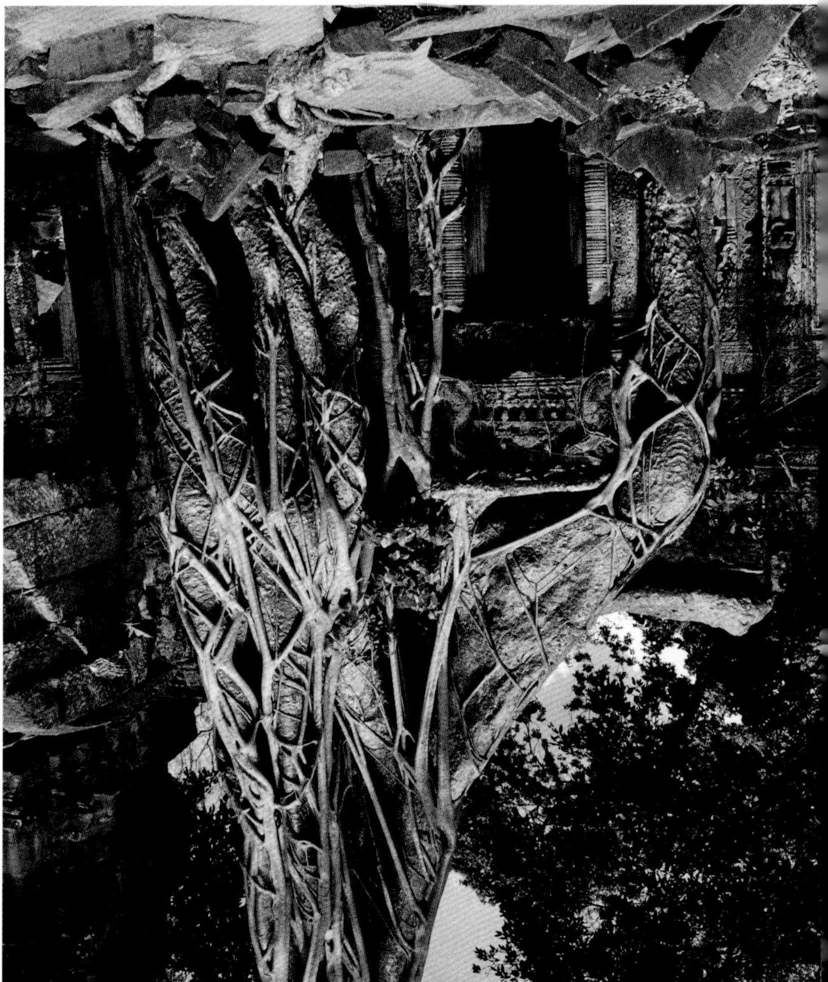

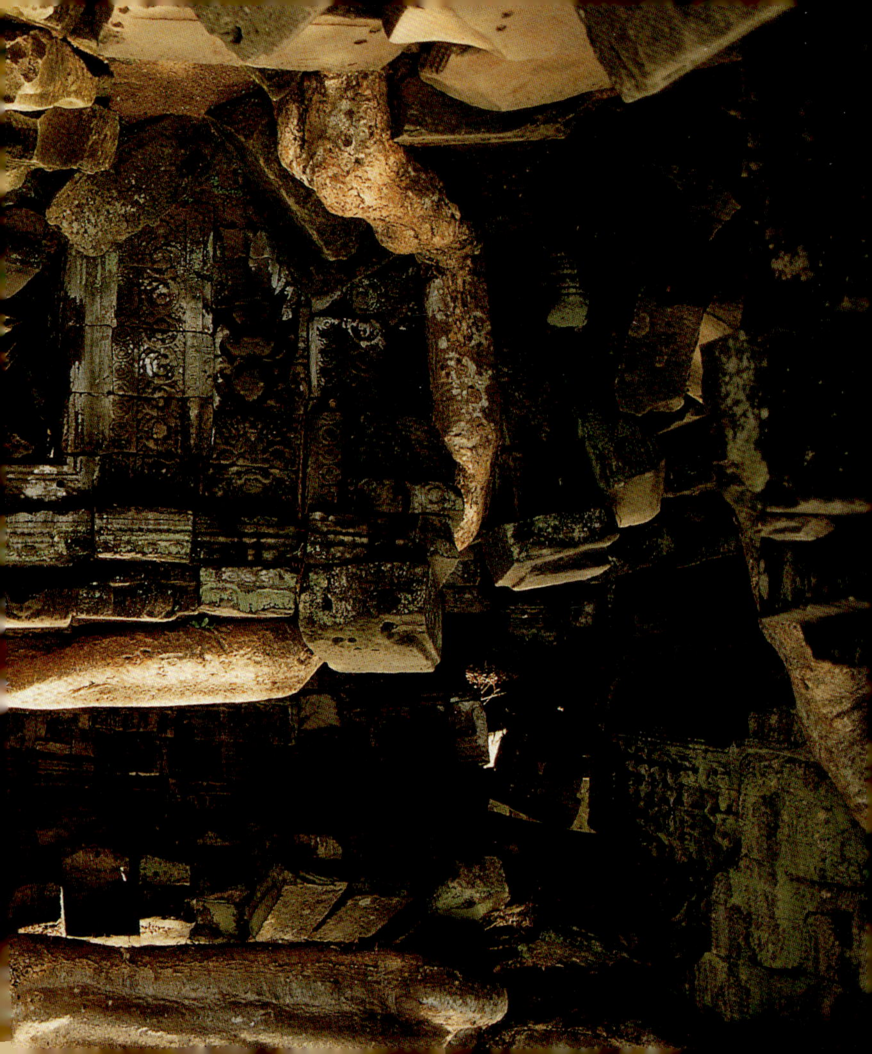

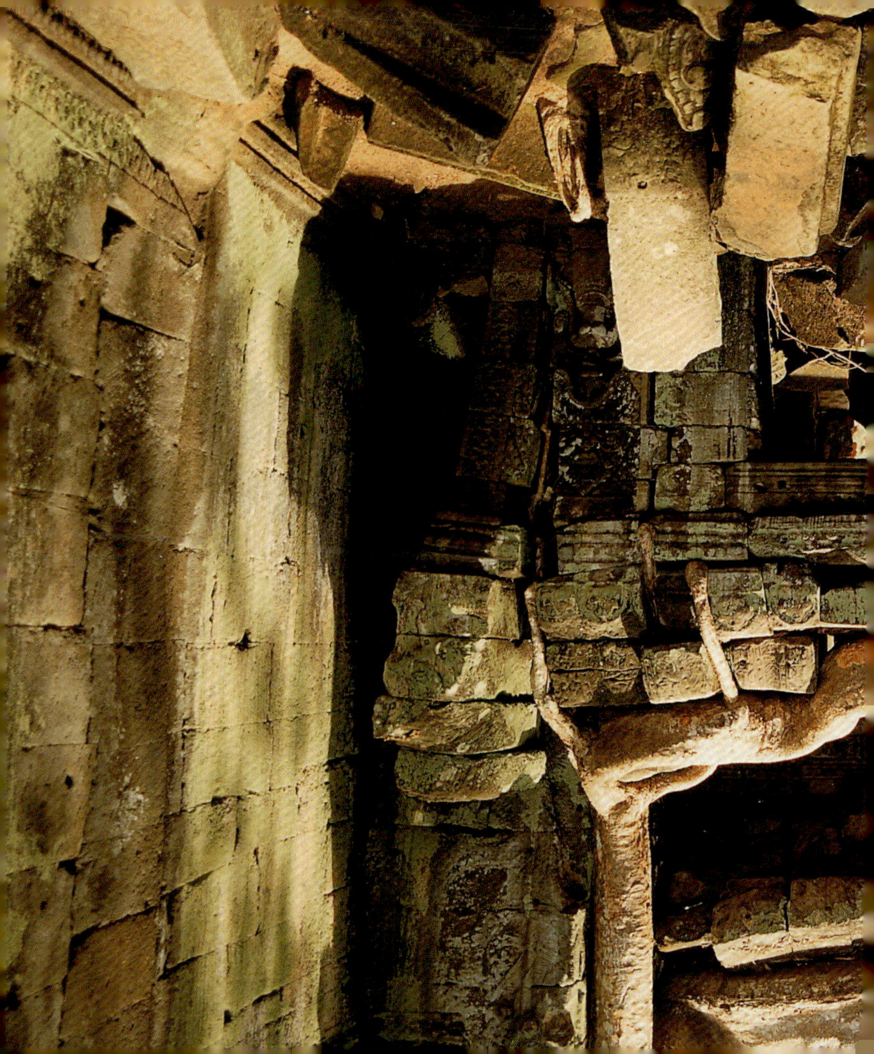

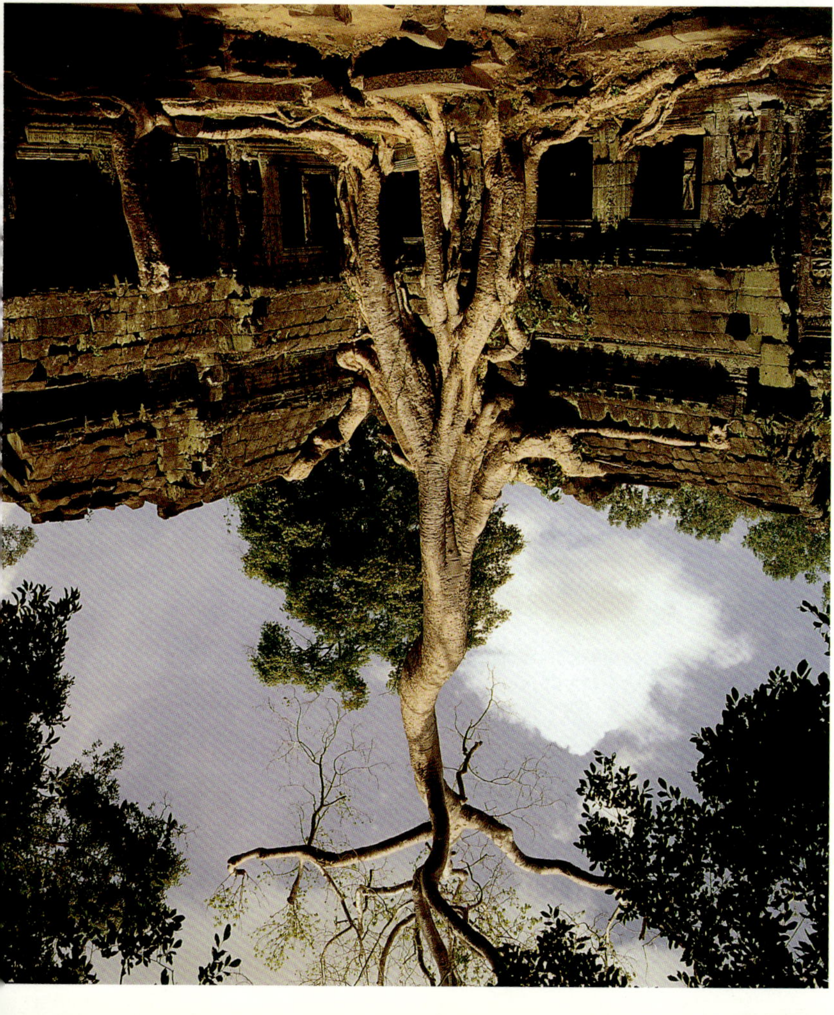

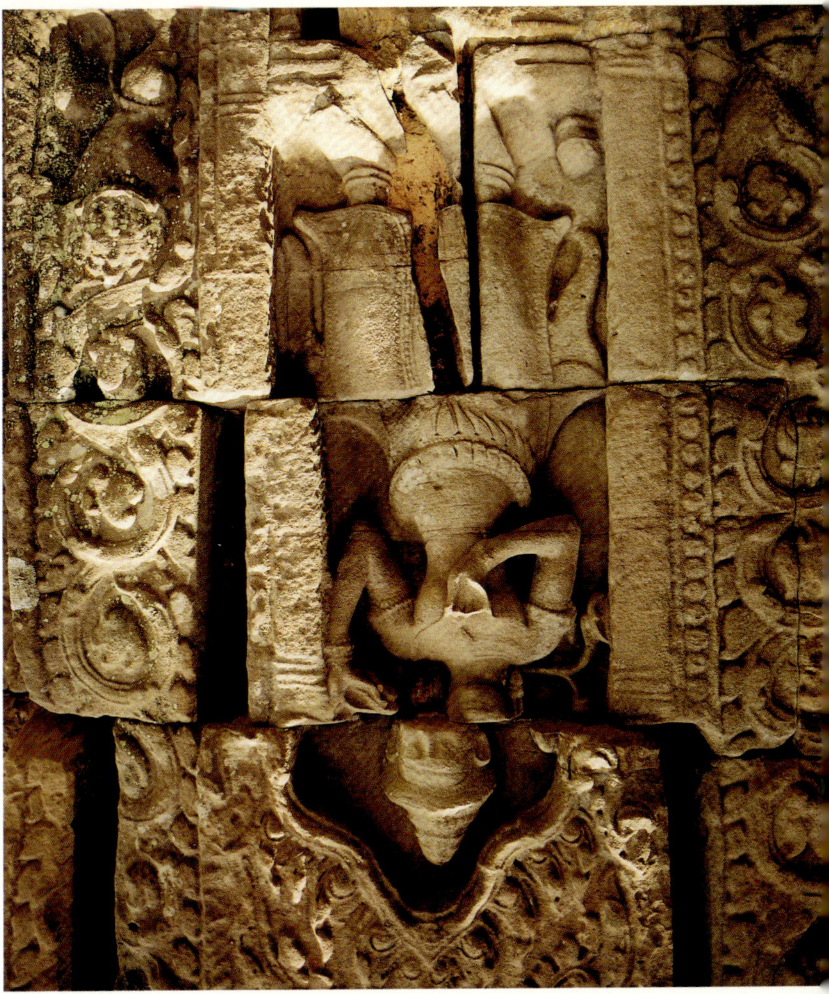

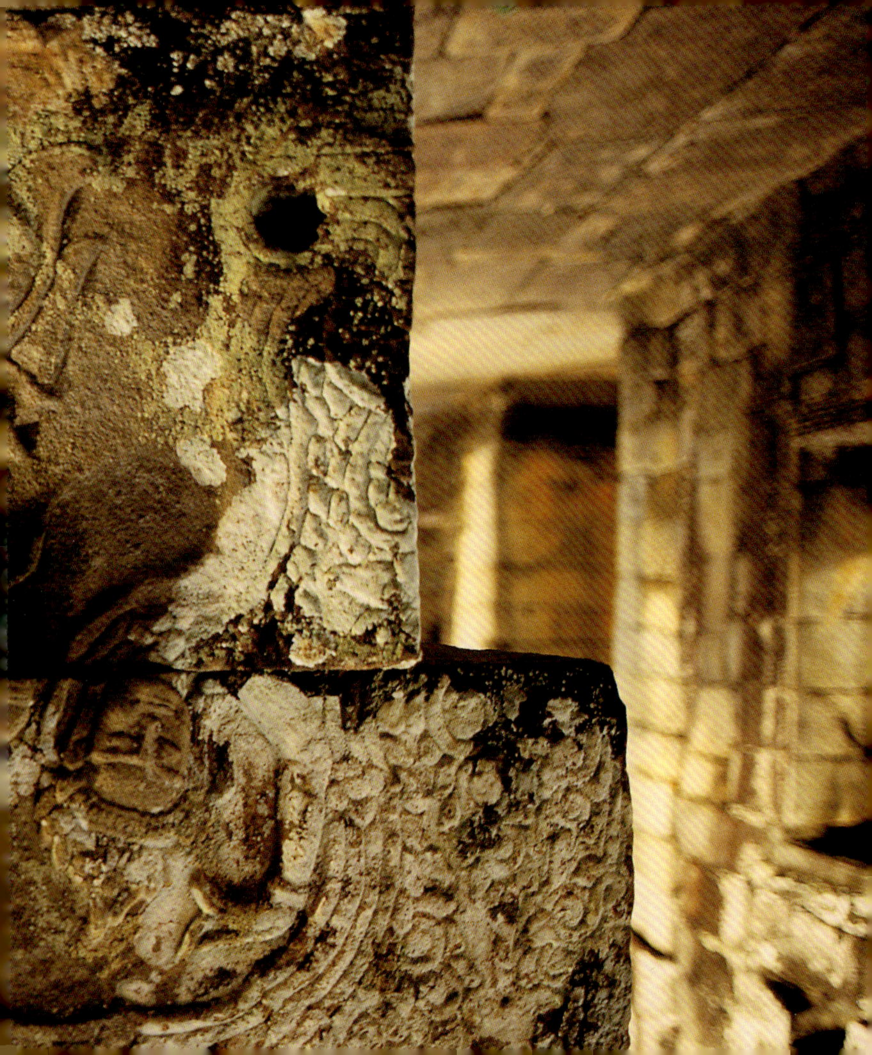

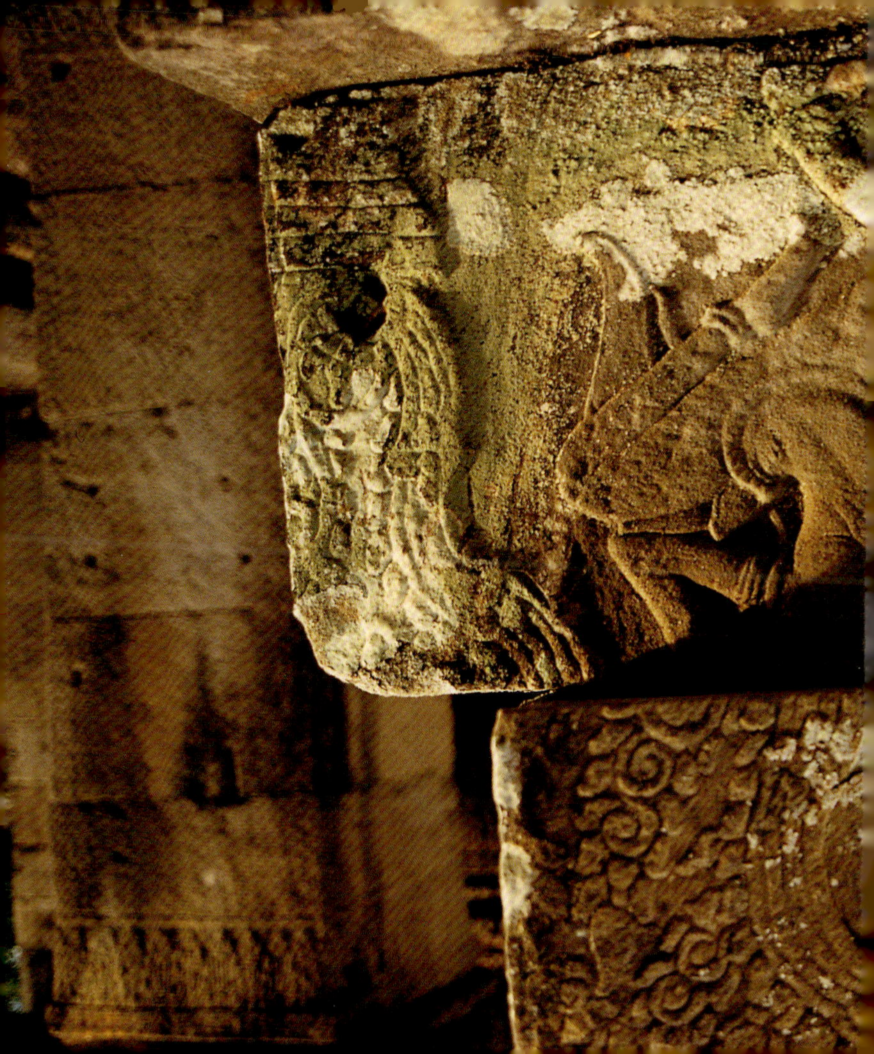

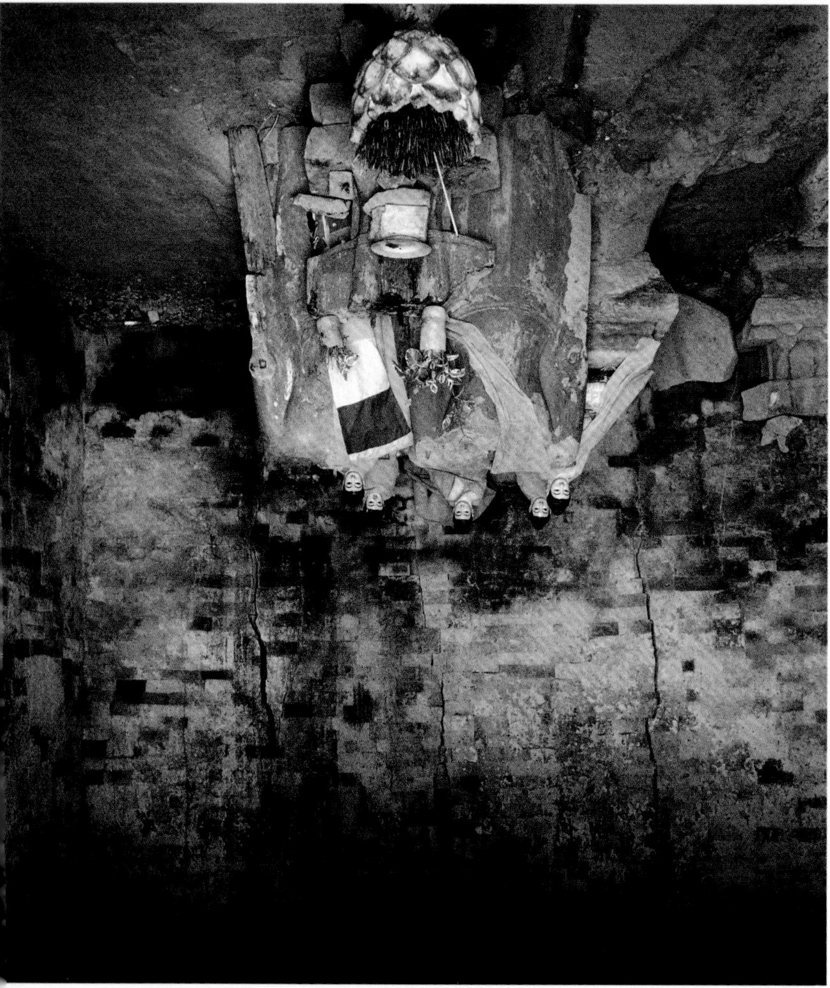

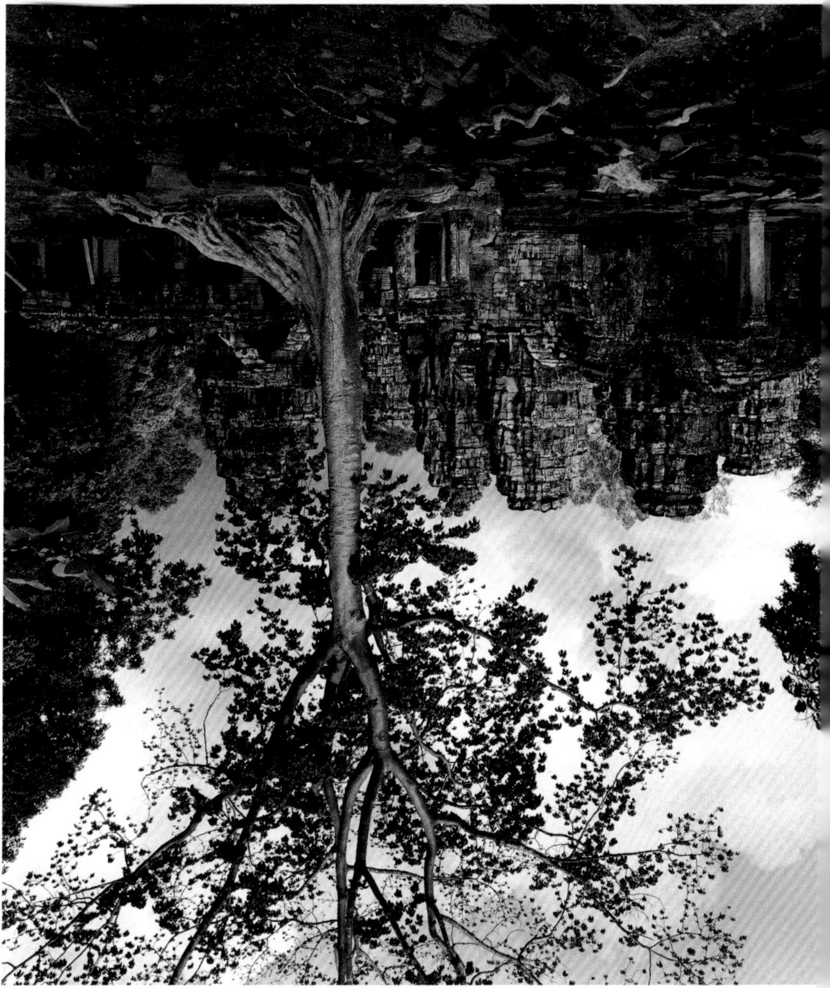

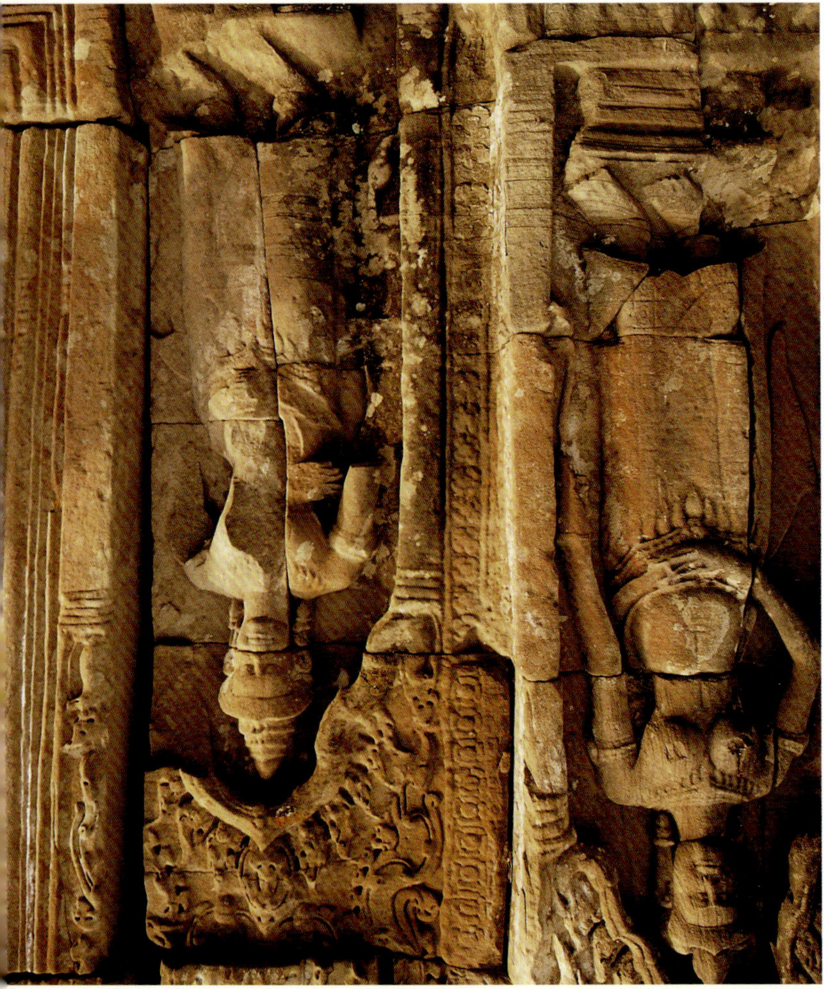

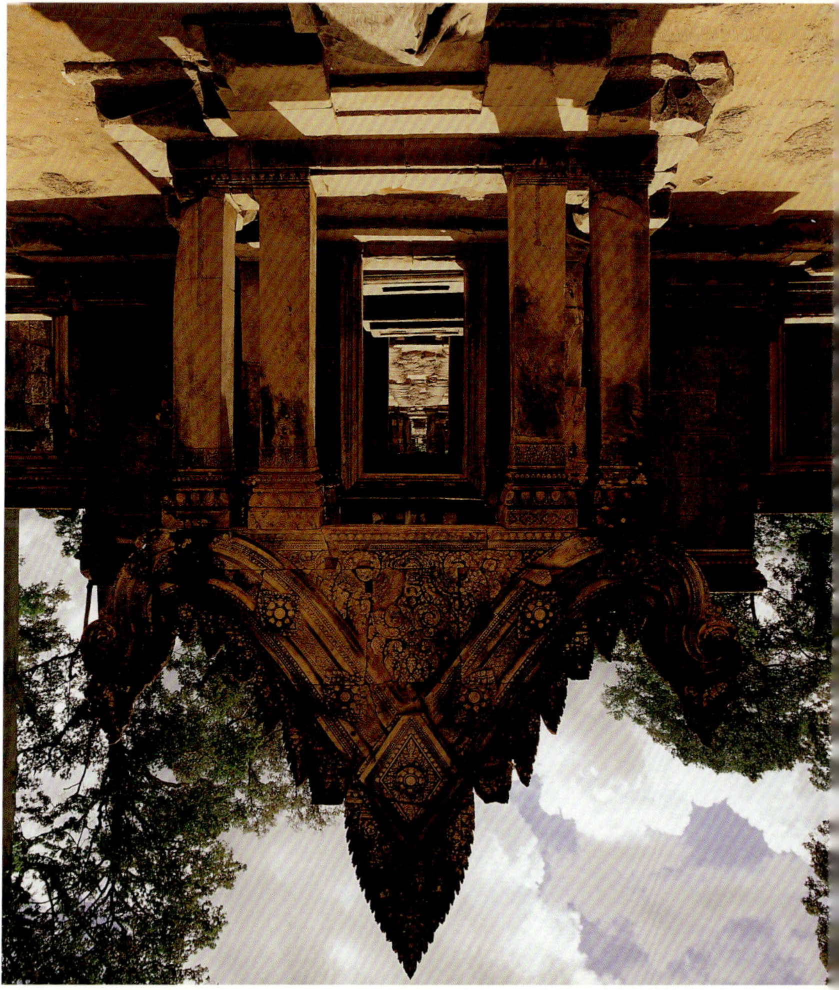

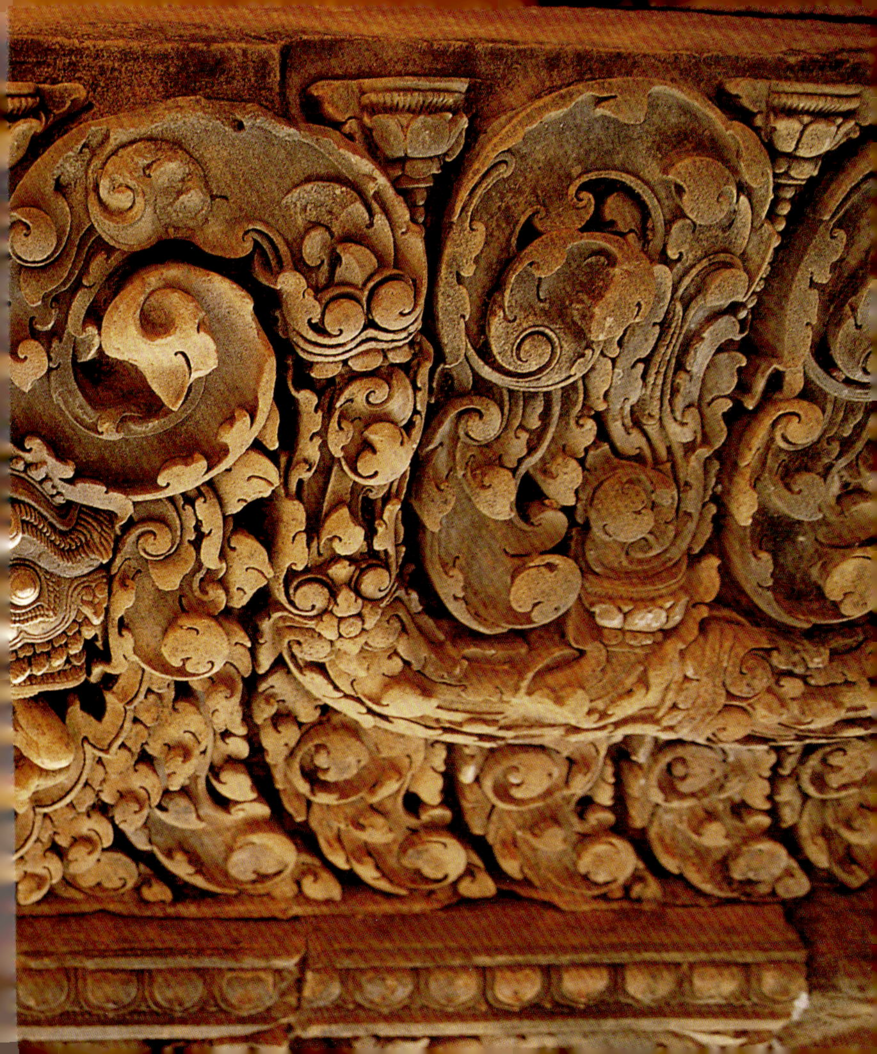

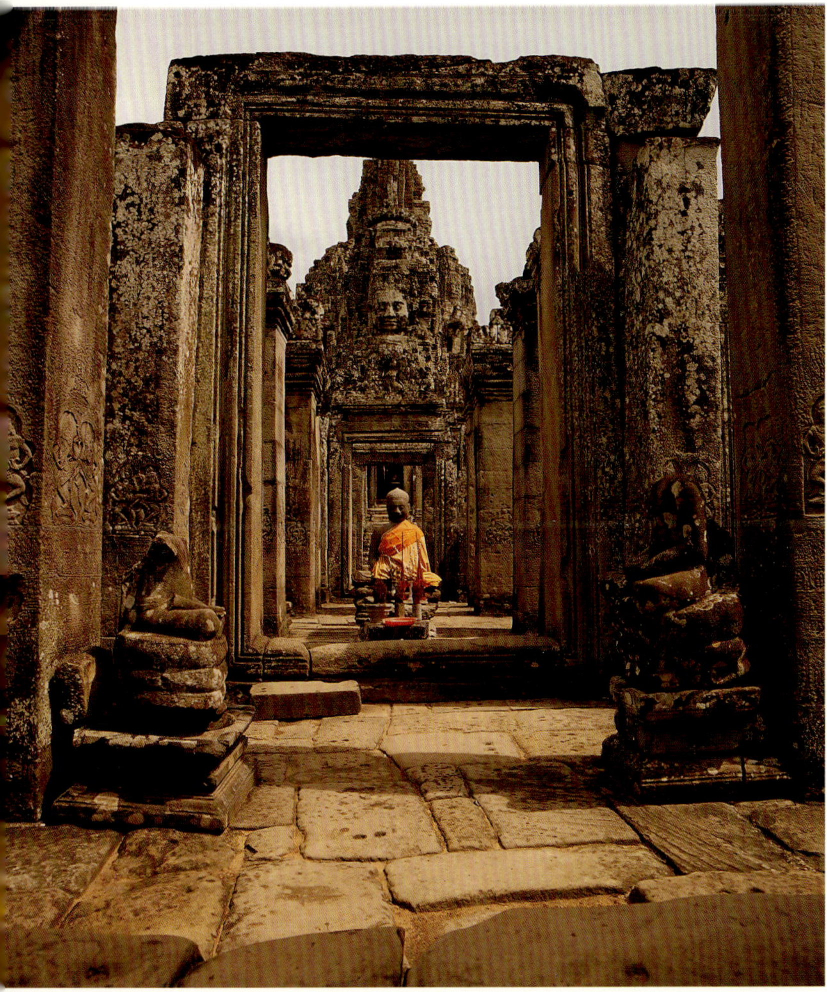

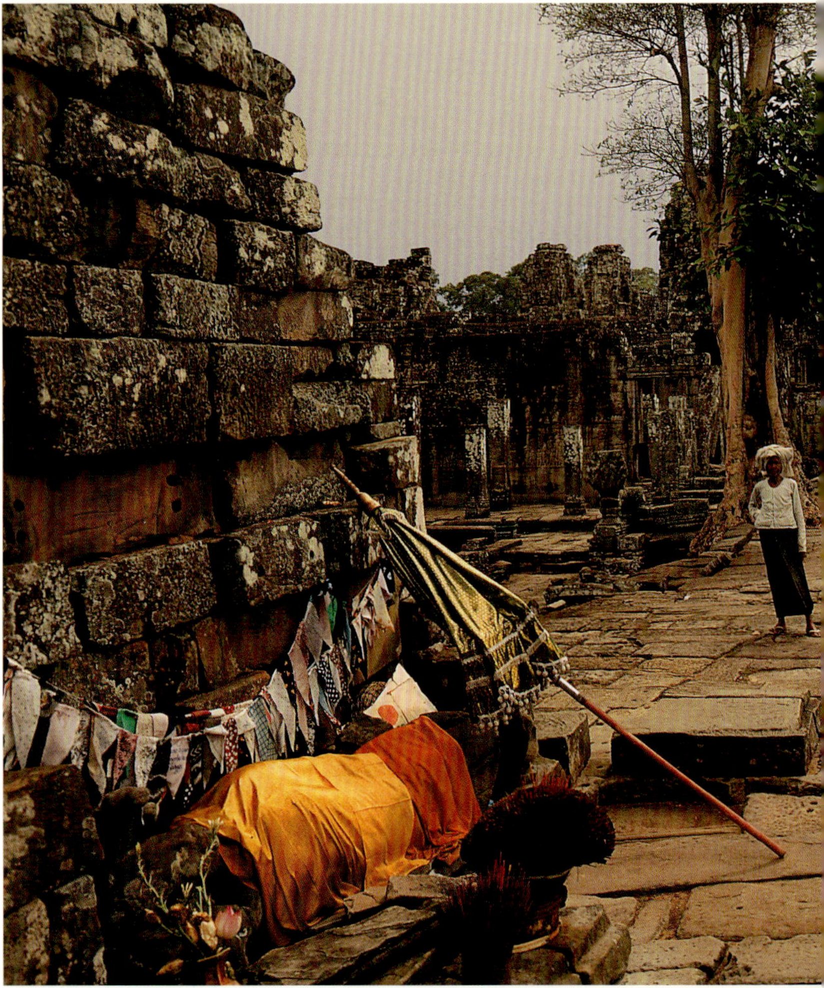

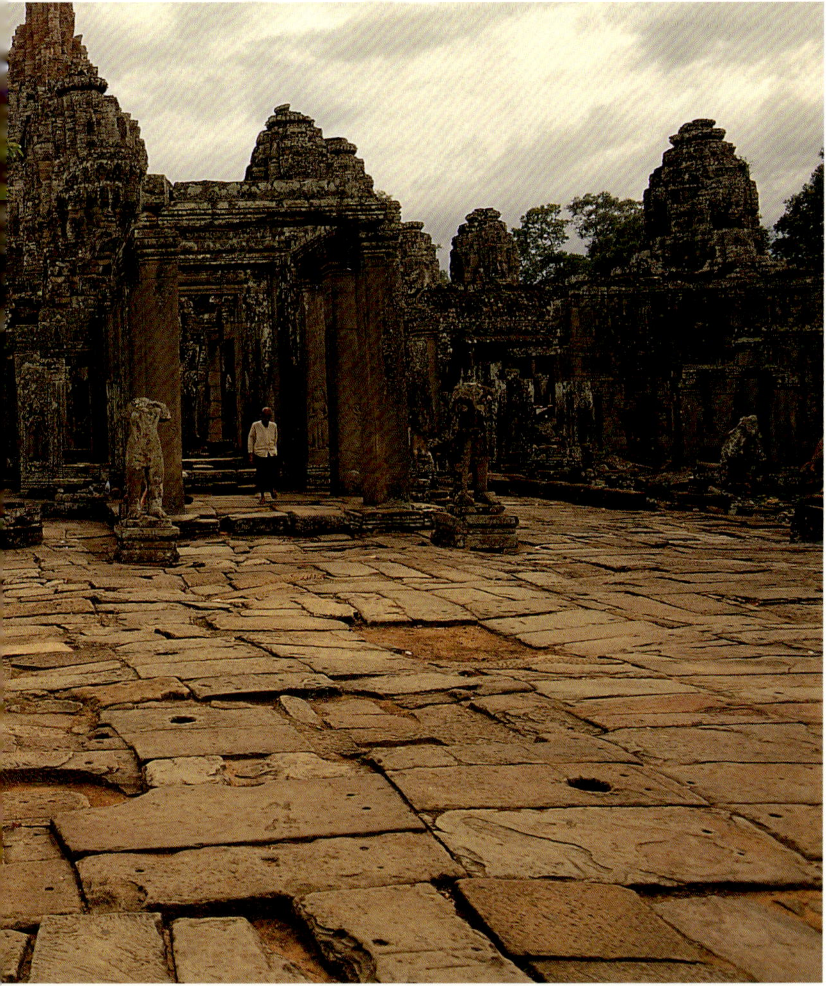

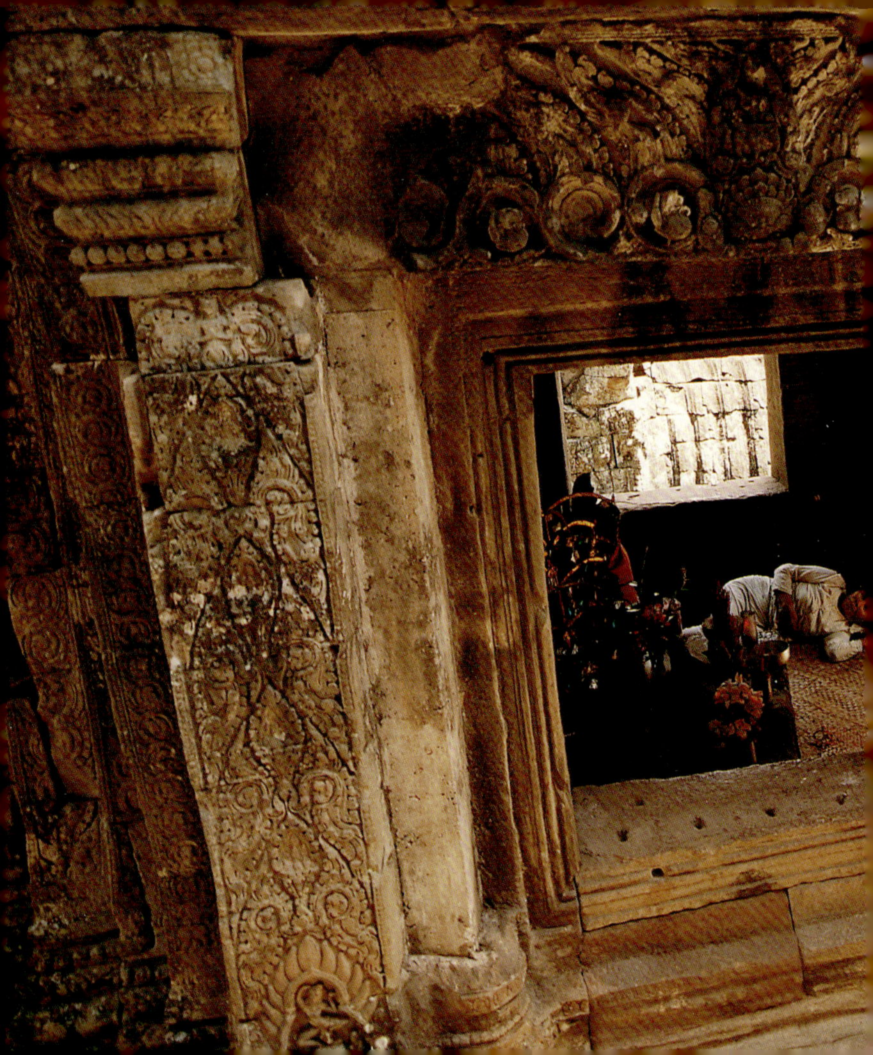

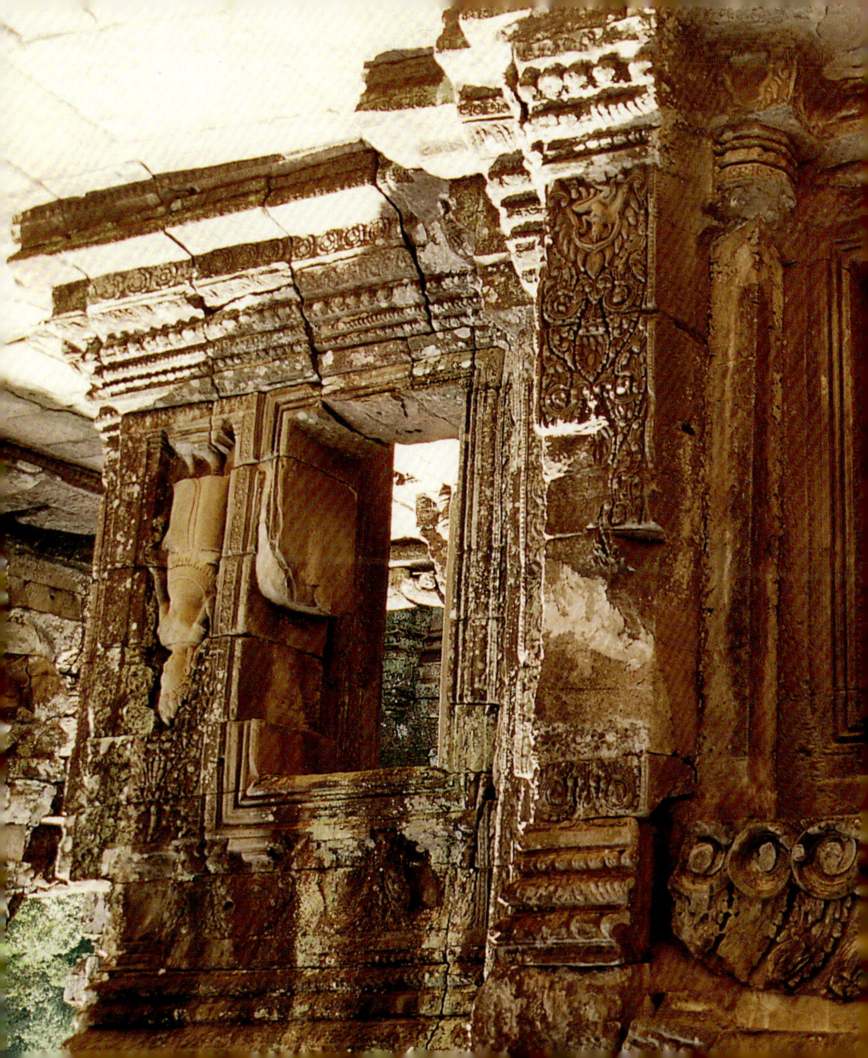

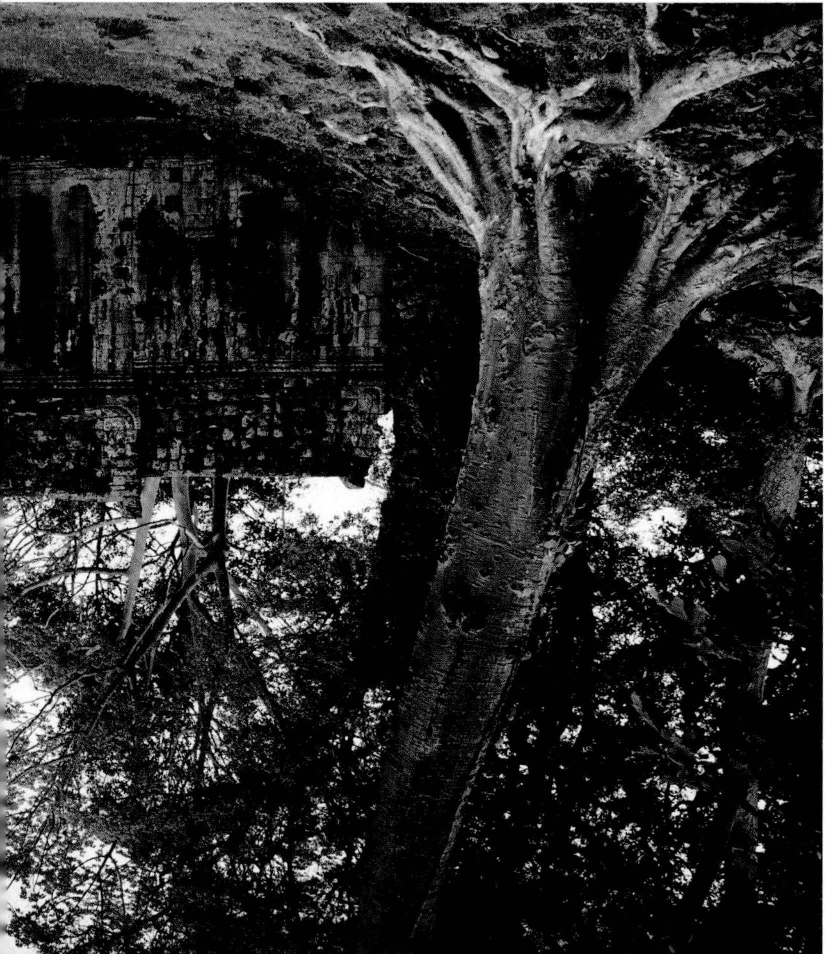

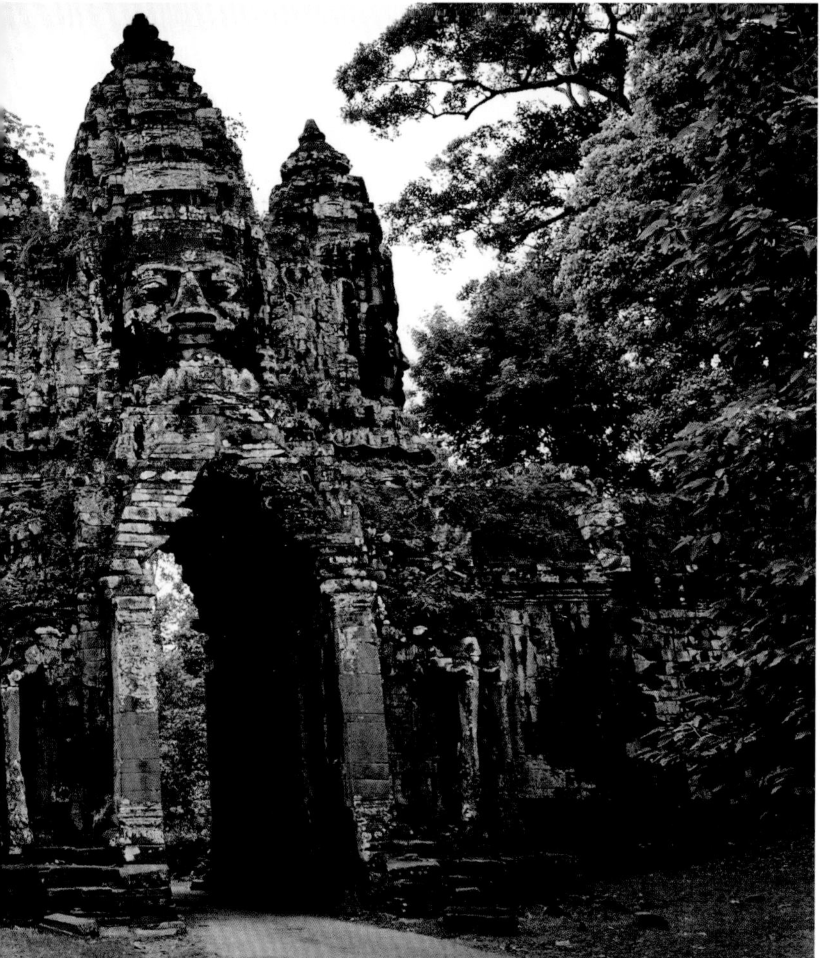

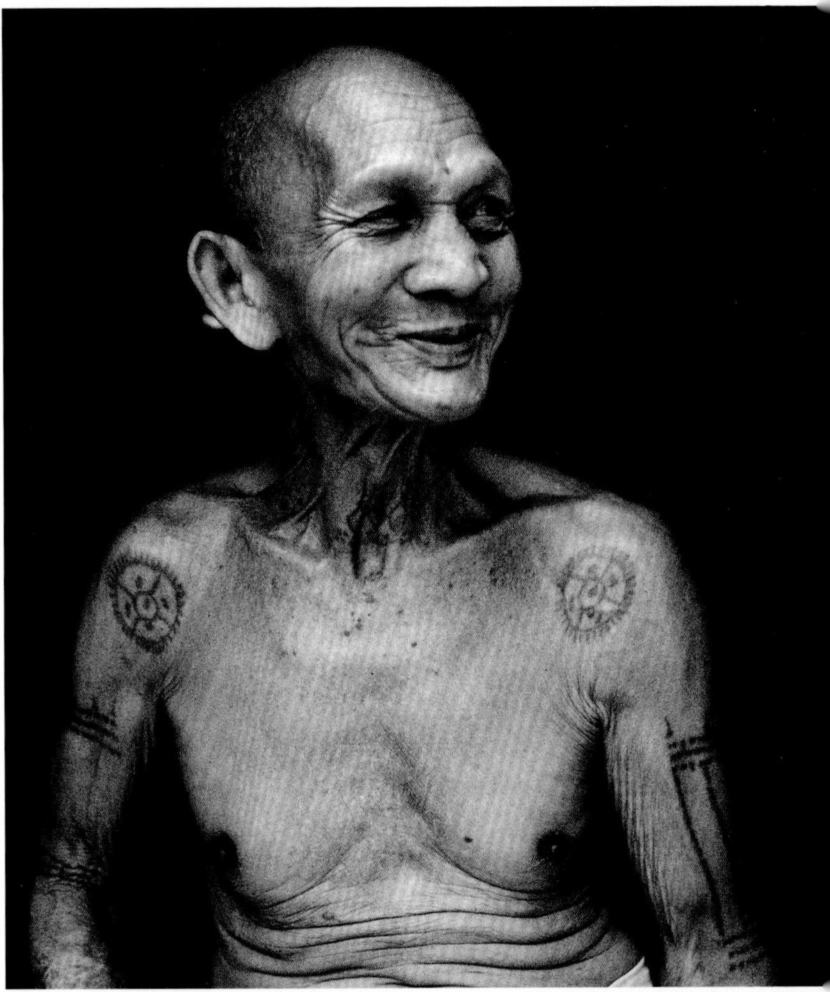

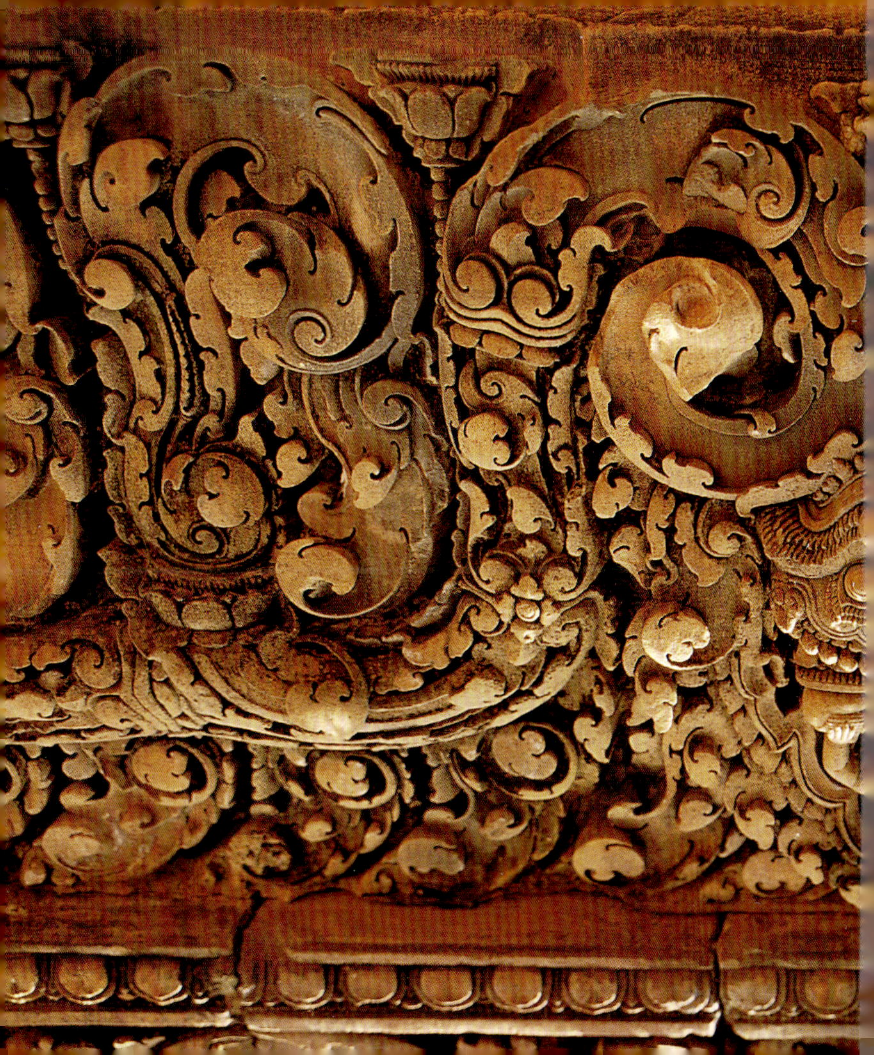

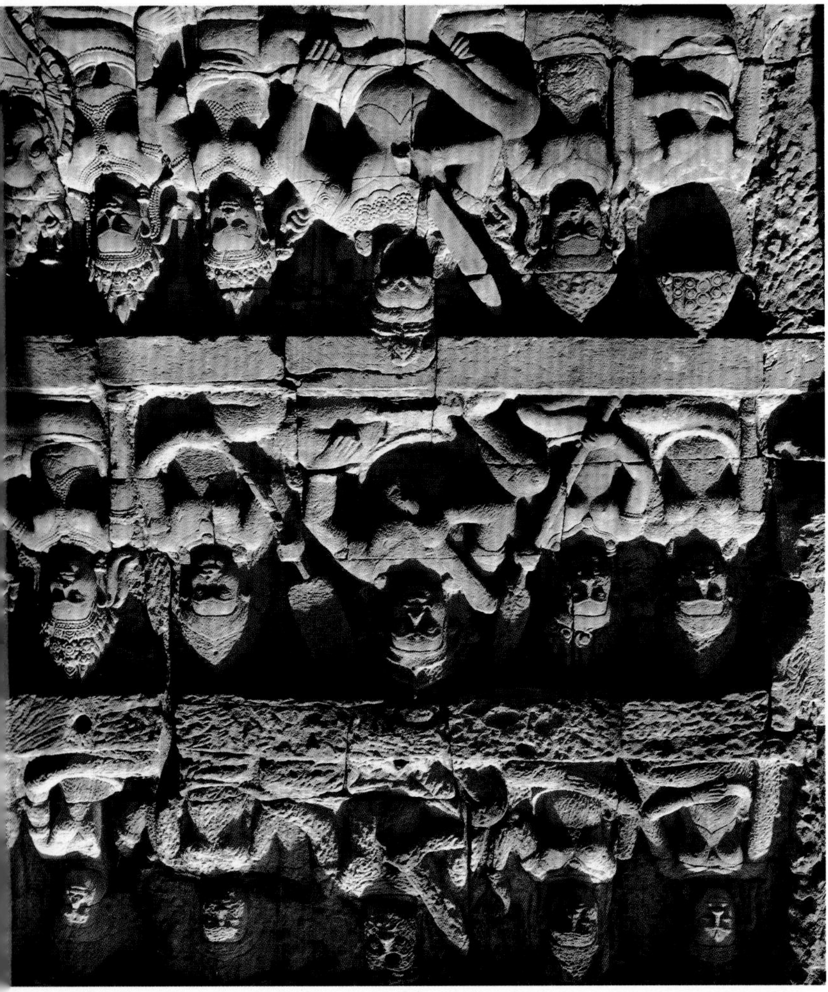

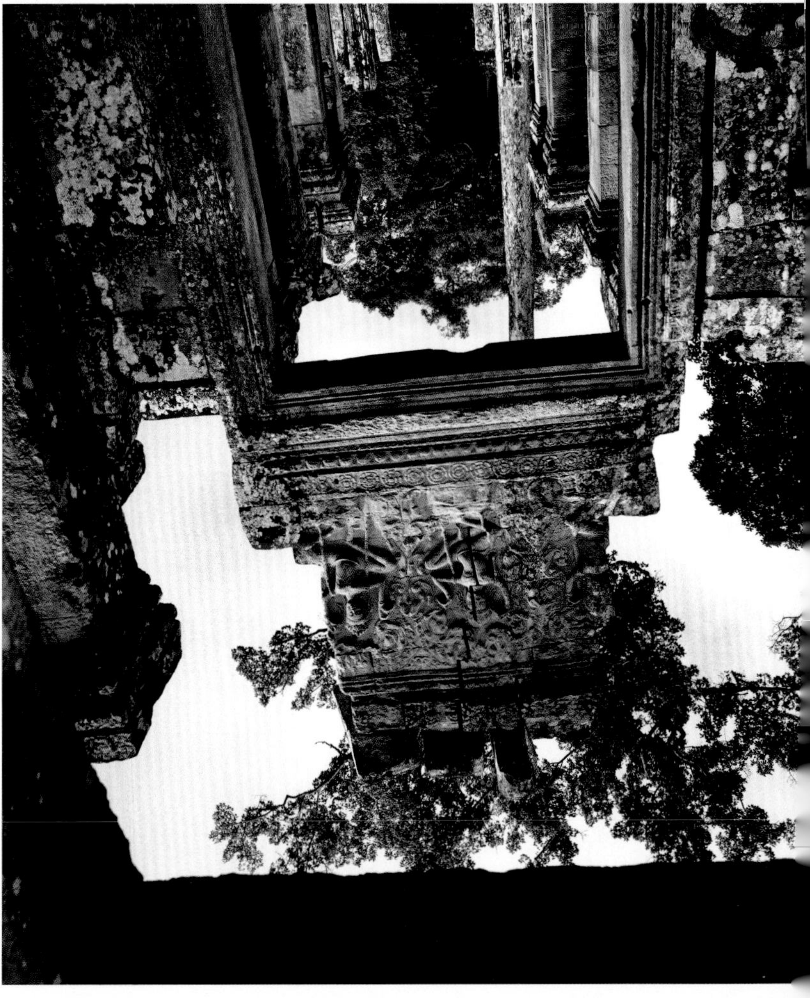

Shambhala Publications, Inc.
Horticultural Hall
300 Massachusetts Avenue
Boston, Massachusetts 02115
www.shambhala.com

To the people of Cambodia,
my grandchildren Adrien and Amandine, and Bernard Cosey.

9 8 7 6 5 4 3 2 1

Printed in Switzerland

Distributed in the United States by Random House, Inc.,
and in Canada by Random House of Canada Ltd

Library of Congress-in-Publication Data

Grandjean, Jean-Pierre, 1950–
Angkor / photographer, Jean-Pierre Grandjean.—1st ed.
p. cm.
ISBN 1-59030-003-0 (hard : alk. paper)
1. Angkor Wat (Angkor)—Pictorial works. 2. Architecture, Khmer—Cambodia—Angkor (Extinct city) 3. Art, Khmer—Cambodia—Angkor (Extinct city) I. Title
DS554.98.A5 G7 2002
959.6—dc21
2002021772

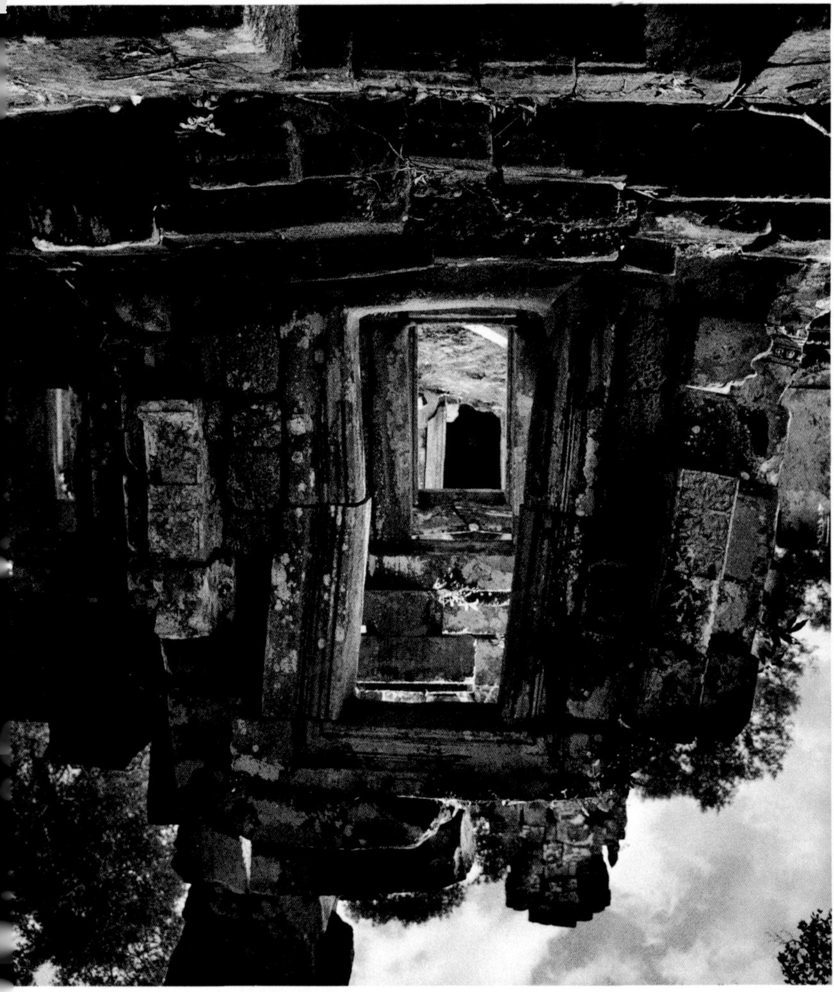

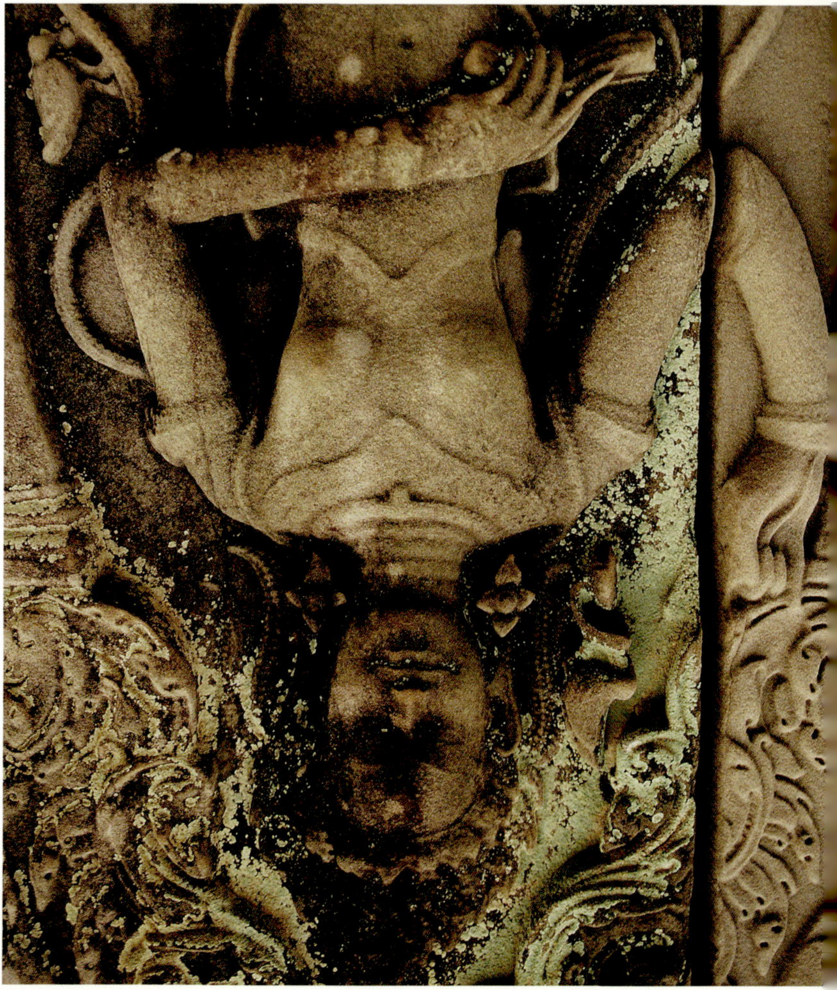

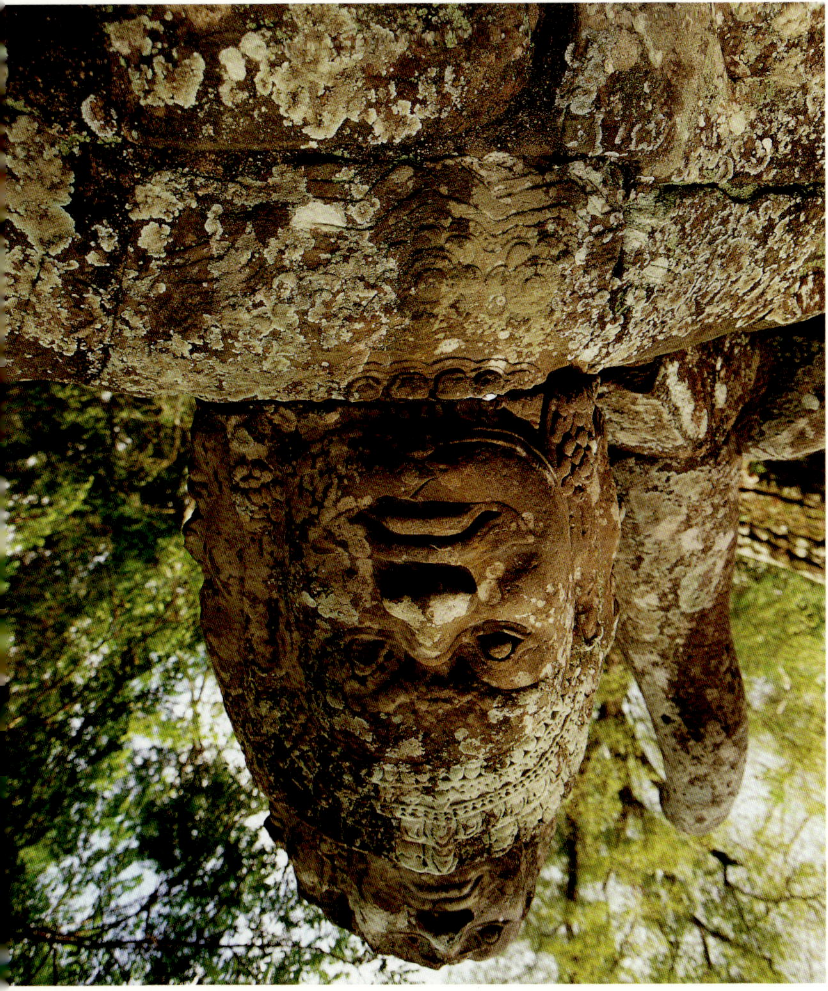

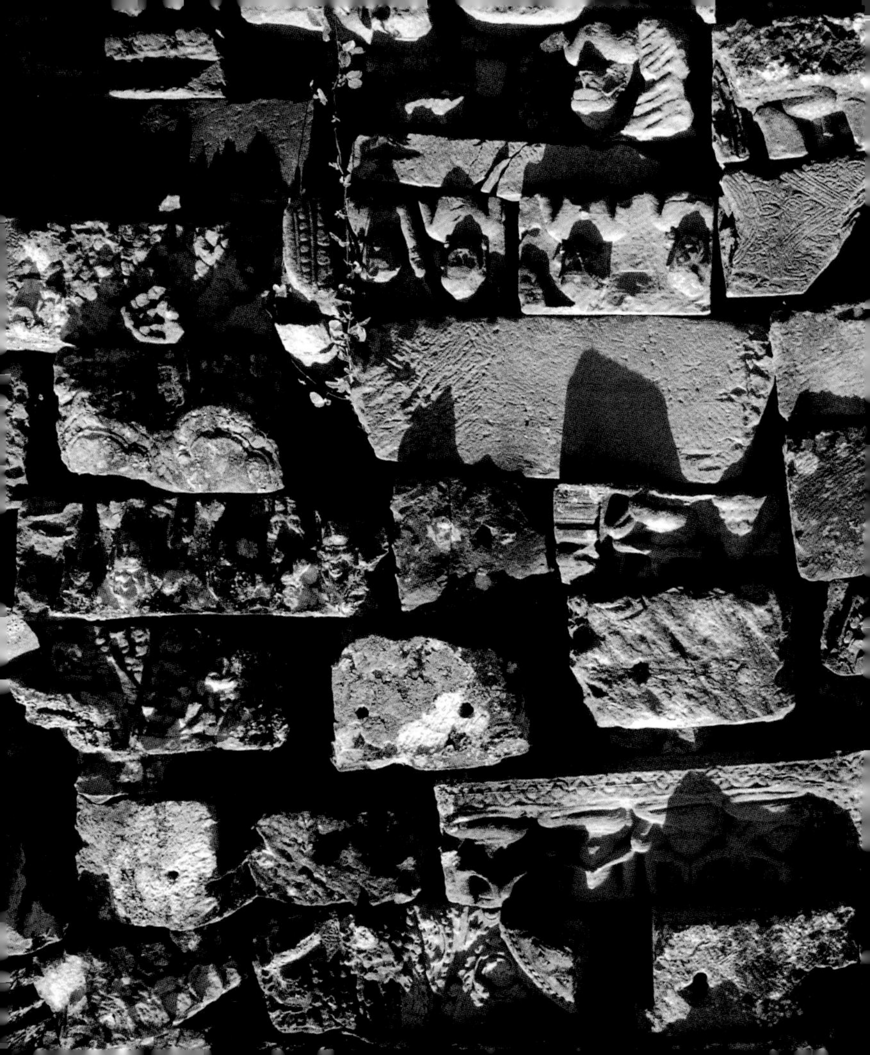